WHEN KATHERINE BREWED,
A PLAY

When Katherine Brewed, a Play

Telling the Story of the Peasants' Revolt and Today's 'New Radical Theatre'

Mark O'Brien and John Cresswell
Play by John Cresswell

OpenBook Publishers

https://openbookpublishers.com

©2025 Mark O'Brien and John Cresswell
©2025 *When Katherine Brewed* by John Cresswell

This work is licensed under a Creative Commons Attribution-NonCommercial-Nonderivatives 4.0 International (CC BY-NC-ND 4.0). This license allows you to share, copy, distribute and transmit the text; to adapt the text for non-commercial purposes of the text providing attribution is made to the authors (but not in any way that suggests that they endorse you or your use of the work). Attribution should include the following information:

Mark O'Brien and John Cresswell (eds), *When Katherine Brewed, a Play: Telling the Story of the Peasants' Revolt and Today's 'New Radical Theatre'*. Cambridge, UK: Open Book Publishers, 2025, https://doi.org/10.11647/OBP.0456

Further details about CC BY-NC licenses are available at http://creativecommons.org/licenses/by-nc/4.0/

All external links were active at the time of publication unless otherwise stated and have been archived via the Internet Archive Wayback Machine at https://archive.org/web

Any digital material and resources associated with this volume are available at https://doi.org/10.11647/OBP.0456#resources

Information about any revised edition of this work will be provided at https://doi.org/10.11647/OBP.0456

Applied Theatre Praxis vol. 4.
ISSN (Print): 2515-0758
ISSN (Digital): 2515-0766

ISBN Paperback 978-1-80511-543-4
ISBN Hardback 978-1-80511-544-1
ISBN PDF 978-1-80511-545-8
ISBN HTML 978-1-80511-547-2
ISBN EPUB 978-1-80511-546-5
DOI: 10.11647/OBP.0456

Cover image: Photo by Step 10 Studio, CC BY NC-ND
Cover design: Jeevanjot Kaur Nagpal

Contents

Telling the Story of the Peasants' Revolt and Today's
'New Radical Theatre' 1

When Katherine Brewed
A Play about the 1381 English Peasants' Revolt 13
Written by John Cresswell

    Cast 13
    Scene 1 15
    Scene 2 21
    Scene 3 35
    Scene 4 36
    Scene 5 40
    Scene 6 40
    Scene 7 41
    Scene 8 42
    Scene 9 43
    Scene 10 44
    Scene 11 45
    Scene 12 54
    Scene 13 56
    Scene 14 58
    Scene 15 59
    Scene 16 60
    Scene 17 62
    Scene 18 64
    Scene 19 65
    Scene 20 73

Scene 21	75
Scene 22	76
Scene 23	78
Scene 24	80
Scene 25	80
Scene 26	84
Scene 27	86
Scene 28	87
Scene 29	88
Scene 30	90
Appendix I: Supporting organisations	93
Appendix II: Permissions	94
Appendix III: Historical Characters	95
Appendix IV: Fictitious Characters	98

Telling the Story of the Peasants' Revolt and Today's 'New Radical Theatre'

Telling the Story of the Peasants' Revolt

The rising of the southeast counties during the long hot summer of 1381 shook the social order of late medieval England. The clamour arose from the introduction of the deeply iniquitous 'third poll tax' on all the population over the age of 14 years. But the issues lay deeper than that and went back much further in time. The moral decay of the church, the refusal to adhere to the restrictions of bondage to the lord's manor, and weariness of constant war all played a role.

Ever since, in verse and in dramatisations, the story of the rebellion and its principal leaders, Wat Tyler, Jack Straw, and John Ball, have been used to convey one or other political message, picking out some aspects over others, either in cautionary warning—predominantly up until the 17th-century—or in celebration during the era of revolutions in England, North America, and France.

The Chronicles

The 'Peasants' Revolt', as it would come to be known in works of Victorian history writing, almost straight away became a source of fascination for poets and playwrights. Storytellers drew upon available accounts from the various chronicles that were written in the years that followed it. But each of these was written with a bias of its own depending upon the standpoint of the chroniclers, their political purpose and the interests of any wealthy patron. Most were unsympathetic to the rebels.

©2025 Mark O'Brien and John Cresswell, CC BY-NC-ND 4.0   https://doi.org/10.11647/OBP.0456.00

So, whereas the *Anonimalle Chronicle*, written during Richard II's reign, portrayed his actions at pivotal moments during the Revolt in a heroic light, the *Knighton's Chronicon* by Henry Knighton favoured his rival for the throne, John of Gaunt. And whilst Jean Froissart in his *Chronicles of England, France, Spain and the Adjoining Countries* (1326–1400) was sympathetic to the English king, the chronicles written after his overthrow by Henry Bolingbroke in 1399 reflected loyalties to the Lancastrian line of inheritance. However, the accounts written by the monks at St Albans Abbey, such as the *Chronica Maiora*, attacked John of Gaunt for his protection of the Wycliffite Lollards. And the *Historia Vitae et Regni Richard II* by the Monk of Evesham portrayed the Essex and Kentish rebels as an unruly mob without rational purpose. Only *The Westminster Chronicle*, based upon accounts of the events in London, whilst condemning the violence of the Revolt, acknowledged the grievances behind it.

The Revolt in Early Literature

The Revolt of 1381 was to quickly enter the 'estate satire' literature of the period, in which the different classes are parodied and the social order upended. As with the chronicles, if there were axes to grind, then they were. In his dream poem *Vox Clamantis*, John Gower added new verse after the rising—'The Visio Anglie'—making the rebels appear in animal form, becoming pigs, dogs, cats, asses, oxen, foxes, birds, frogs, and flies that lay siege to New Troy (the City of London). These demented animals have all forgotten their proper place and broken free of their ordained roles as creatures of nature or beasts of burden. The result, the reader is assured, can only be the end of all that is good. In Geoffrey Chaucer's 'The Nun's Priest's Tale' of *The Canterbury Tales*, reference to Jack Straw, the Essex leader of the Revolt, is used to convey the sense of panic and disorder caused by the taking of the cockerel Chauntecleer by the fox. And William Langland, whose epic poem *Piers Plowman* had inspired the rebels, later changed parts of the poem to disassociate it from the Revolt.

Revolution, Radicals and the Socialist Tradition

The cautionary use of the story of 1381 continued into the 17th-century. The play *The Life and Death of Jack Straw* authored (probably) by George

Peele and printed in 1593, was performed in the City of London guild pageants of the early 1600s. In it, John Ball, the spiritual inspiration of the rising, leads Jack Straw and his followers to disaster.

During the English Civil War, it was used as a source of metaphors and signifiers in the literature of both the royalist and anti-royalist causes. In *The Idol of the Clownes*,[1] written by the royalist John Cleveland, 'Wat Tyler' can be read as Oliver Cromwell and the 'rebels' as Cromwell's army, with the author's disdain for the 'self-interest' of the former intended really for the latter. The most radical elements of insurgent Protestantism, however, identified with the memory of the Revolt.

In the period of the Jacobite risings and the American Revolution, references to the Revolt appear increasingly in popular pamphlets and journals. But it is with the radicalism inspired by the French Revolution that we see it become more widely known and celebrated. For Thomas Paine, rebuffing the criticisms levelled against the memory of the Revolt by the anti-revolutionary conservative Edmund Burke, its roots lay in the injustices of the time. Whilst Burke condemned the common mass, separated from their 'proper chieftains', as no more than 'deserters and vagabonds',[2] Paine condemned the 'base action of the Court'[3] and called for the erection of a statue to Wat Tyler at Smithfields, where he had been assassinated. And, influenced by Paine, a young Robert Southey was to praise the rebels of 1381 in passionate verse in his *Wat Tyler: A Dramatic Poem*. In the poem's dialogue, Southey has John Ball voice the truth of the rising as one against poverty and oppression:

> *And there will be a time, when this great truth*
> *Shall be confess'd – be felt by all mankind.*
> *The electric truth shall run from man to man,*
> *And the blood cemented pyramid of greatness*
> *Shall fall before the flash!*[4]

---

1   Also titled *Insurrection of Wat the Tyler with his Priests Baal and Straw*.
2   Burke, E. (1983), 'An Appeal from the New to the Old Whigs' quoted in Dobson, R. (1983), *The Peasants' Revolt of 1381*, MacMillan. P. 392
3   Paine, T. (1983), 'The Rights of Man' quoted in Dobson, R. (1983), *The Peasants' Revolt of 1381*, MacMillan. P. 396
4   Southey, R. (1983), 'Wat Tyler: A Dramatic Poem' quoted in Dobson, R. (1983), *The Peasants' Revolt of 1381*, MacMillan. P. 398

In the 1840s, the image of Wat Tyler appeared on Chartist banners, and the Greenwich 'Wat Tyler Brigade' dubbed him 'the great and original Chartist'. And, in the later socialist literature of the 19th-century, the story of Wat Tyler and his followers was used again for its message of political hope and inspiration. In his *Lives of English Popular Leaders of the Middle Ages* (1875), Charles Edmund Maurice explored the class conflict that drove the rising. And in *A Dream of John Ball* (1888), William Morris as the narrator goes back in time to speak to John Ball in his prison cell after the suppression of the Revolt. He tells Ball about the end of feudalism, the rise of the guilds, and the industrial age they heralded. And they reflect together on the reasons why the new age of freedom and equality has not yet come to pass. But above all, Morris presses upon Ball the importance of the rising and the beacon of hope it has lit that will shine down the centuries and assures him that he shall not be forgotten.

In the 20th-century, the polarised nature of accounts of the rising continued. In another leftist literary treatment, Florence Converse's historical novel *Long Will* (1903), the chief protagonists of the Revolt appear in a positive light—and with some poetic license—whilst in Charles Oman's *The Great Revolt of 1381* (1906), Wat Tyler is portrayed as a demagogue and a 'mob orator' with an 'insolent tongue'.

A later generation of socialist historians was to take the story of the 1381 Revolt as subject matter, some seeking to trace a distinctively English radical tradition. These works were to develop the embrace of the rising by the political left. Hyman Fagan's *Nine Days That Shook England*, published by the Left Book Club (associated with the Communist Party of Great Britain), appeared in 1938. Accounts that emphasised the agency of the rebels, as distinct from the economic determinist tendency apparent in much communist history writing, began to appear in the post-Second-World-War era. From the Trotskyist tradition came *The Peasants' Revolt of 1381* (1950) by Reg Groves and Philip Lindsay. And Rodney Hilton's *Bond Men Made Free* (1973) placed the Revolt in its wider European context as the first of a wave of millenarian movements that were to reach as far as Bohemia.

Our Approach to the Story of the Revolt

Our treatment of the story of 1381 draws upon this latter tradition. Mark, in his *When Adam Delved and Eve Span: A History of the Peasants' Revolt* (2004) sides completely with the rebels, emphasising the huge injustices of the time. Although its class composition was more complex than the term 'Peasants' Revolt' suggests, the rising was driven above all by the experience of economic exploitation and social insult levelled at the land workers of 14th-century England. Our approach also brings out the hypocrisy, venality, and fickleness of the rulers of the period and their ecclesiastical lackeys. Moreover, the story for us provides a universal metaphor for the social anger and thirst for freedom that has characterised countless liberation movements since that time. In the UK, when the movement against the 'poll tax' of the Margaret Thatcher government erupted, many a speaker at protests invoked the memory of Wat Tyler.

To bring the story of the Peasants' Revolt to a wider audience, we decided to produce a play, bringing together John's dramaturgical skills and Mark's knowledge of the historical story together in collaboration. The result is *When Katherine Brewed*.

The 'New Radical Theatre' and What It Means Today

Every country has its TV soap dramas based upon working-class life. In the UK, there is the BBC's *EastEnders*. Set in the fictitious London borough of Walford, the characters are no-nonsense, unsentimental, and tough. But no-one in Walford ever joins a union, goes on strike, or organises a counterdemonstration against fascist thugs coming into their area.

That's because, while *EastEnders* tells stories about working-class people, every aspect of its production—scripts, story arcs, recording, casting, direction, and editing—is controlled by a multi-billion-pound state broadcaster that ultimately serves its class interests; in other words, a tiny minority of society producing culture for the great majority who have no say. As Walter Benjamin conveys in his 1934 essay 'The Author as Producer' commenting on Brecht's Epic Theatre, the productive technique behind the performance tells us as much about its politics as the explicit narrative content. It is only by making the mechanics of the creative processes involved transparent that we reveal the full meaning of the drama.

For theatre (and art in general) to be 'working-class', it must be funded, produced, and above all artistically controlled by that oppressed and exploited class, making stories about itself, performed by itself, to itself. But to be 'radical', these processes must intervene in the struggle to end capitalism.

There is a rich and ancient tradition of theatre and spectacle created by oppressed people. The European medieval Charivari was one way that the poorest members of a village community could ridicule and embarrass their so-called 'betters' with their grievances. With clanging pots and 'rough music' a crowd would seek to humiliate the offender, often manhandling them, parading them through the village and even dunking them or worse. And the appointed Lord of Misrule gave a yearly opportunity during the Christmas period for the downtrodden to mock and upset their masters. These rituals could act as pressure valves that would permit ordinary people to blow off steam and, so local rulers hoped, prevent genuine revolutions like the one that is the subject of our play. We see this too in the concept of the Fool, an apparently simple soul with license to speak truth to power and potentially subvert it. That was certainly how Shakespeare used this figure.

In every generation, theatre has been a contested ground between the classes; bourgeois theatre seeking to entertain an audience for an evening; working-class theatre seeking to educate and agitate for a better world. And for each generation, the meaning of 'radical theatre' is recreated. In the early decades of the 20th century, and notably in periods of heightened social and political struggle, types of theatre emerged that consciously attempted to raise awareness of class. There was the Proletarian Children's Theatre of the Latvian Bolshevik, Asja Lacis, who declared the revolutionary content of the 'New Tendencies in Theatre' in her 1921 essay of that title. Bertolt Brecht's epic Smokers' Theatre attempted to create the atmosphere of the boxing match, where the audience would smoke, drink, and revel in a way quite at odds with the conventional expectations of audience behaviour. Brecht used distancing devices aimed at preventing an audience from dwelling so much on *what* was happening, to focus instead on *why*. In contrast to naturalistic drama, he did not intend that audience members would leave the theatre happy with 'That's alright then' dramatic resolutions. Rather, Brecht wanted them dissatisfied, angry, thoughtful, and more determined to act on the world.

In the 1930s, the Workers' Theatre Movement saw a proliferation of 'Red' regional theatre groups around Britain, such as the Salford Red Megaphones, the Sunderland Red Magnets and the Merseyside Left Theatre, their anti-capitalist and anti-fascist productions announced and reported in the movement's publication *Red Stage*. In the post-Second-World-War era, Jerzy Grotowski's Poor Theatre, in contrast with the Rich Theatre that tried to emulate the lavish costume and settings of TV and cinema production, stripped sets down to the barest essentials.

During the militant upsurge and subsequent reaction of the 1960s and 1970s, Dario Fo in Italy (*Accidental Death of an Anarchist, Trumpets and Raspberries*) and Augusto Boal's Theatre of the Oppressed forum theatre in Brazil continued this tradition. In the US, from the late 1960s and onwards over the next two decades, the work of Living Theatre (founded in the 1940s), Performance Group, Open Theatre, Bridge Collective, Firehouse Collective, Ridiculous Theatre Company and San Francisco Mime Troupe, amongst many others, combined in the 'New Radical Theatre' movement of that era, creating a type of theatre that was experimental in form, diverse in participation, and current in its chosen political topics. And on both sides of the Atlantic, these decades also saw important developments in women's theatre, black theatre, and gay and lesbian theatre, and, from the 1980s onwards, disability theatre. In the 1990s and 2000s, the emergence of trans theatre tracked the rise of the movement for trans and nonbinary rights and liberation.

On the socialist left in the UK, there was the radical theatre company 7/84, founded in 1971.[5] At its high point, the English and Scottish branches toured the seminal *The Cheviot, the Stag and the Black, Black Oil*[6] by John McGrath, and other politically aware productions, to working class communities not catered for by mainstream theatre, sometimes

---

5   At this time in the UK, 7% of the population owned 84% of the land.
6   McGrath, J. (1974), *The Cheviot, the Stag and the Black, Black Oil*, West Highland Publishing Co.

performing the play in factories. In 1974 came Banner Theatre, which emerged from the counterculture of the 1960s, pioneering the method of 'actuality', drawing upon the voices of working-class people and developing the 'verbatim theatre' that became influential beyond the UK. Those decades also saw experiments in the democracy of devised theatre; important examples being the Joint Stock and Greenwich and Lewisham Young People's Theatre (GLYPT) companies, as well as 'interventionist' and community drama groups like the Belfast Community Theatre and the Belfast People's Theatre on the Ballymurphy Estate, West Belfast and the Dissident and Community Theatre in Sheffield.

By the early 1990s, the hostile climate created by the Tory government for any type of left-wing art form meant the end of stable financing for radical theatre and the collapse of revenue funding for anti-establishment theatre companies. Since that time, radical theatre has been forced to look far more to sources of support from within the trade-union and left-activist movements. Today, the intensive commercialisation of city centres, with rising costs for the renting and hire of suitable performance spaces, has only increased the pressure.

However, the impoverished condition of left radical theatre, never adequately funded of course, has generated a resourcefulness rooted in determination to represent the truth of working-class life and history. The example of Banner Theatre particularly, which emerged from this crisis to continue its work in partnership with trade unions, provides a model of survival for working-class theatre today. And whilst those who work so hard to continue the cultural legacy of radical drama know well the never-ending quest for funding, the results are productions that retain their left-wing political edge and are undimmed by the coldness of the funding bodies of the capitalist state.

Here we present our own *When Katherine Brewed*. In creative process and final form, it relates to these radical traditions. As class-conscious activists, we have used democratic methods to tell a story from the perspective of the exploited workers of late medieval England. We celebrate their victories, draw lessons from their final defeat, and, above all, encourage critical participation in the struggles to come.

How *When Katherine Brewed* Was Produced

Political Context and Adaptability

Context is all-important for the production and performance of *When Katherine Brewed*.

> By the late 1370s, thirty-odd years of economic, biological and ecological crisis, not to mention disastrous foreign wars —Am I ringing any bells here? — is producing cracks in the ancient feudal system of oppression and exploitation.
> —The Fool, Scene One, *When Katherine Brewed*

The period we are living in resonates with that of the 1381 Peasants' Revolt. A strangely similar conjunction of crises to that which we see today led to this tremendous uprising that nearly overthrew the entire system of feudal exploitation. And although the story has never been completely forgotten, and whilst there was a revival of interest during the period of Thatcher's 'poll tax' in the 1980s, still, it remains a relatively unknown chapter of resistance against oppression.

Lessons stand out for those of us trying to build such a movement today. Resistance does not leap simply from oppression; rather, patient explanation and planning are needed. Ordinary people are capable of extraordinary feats of self-organisation when the crisis comes. Rulers will do whatever they believe is necessary to survive, including using the deepest deceits and the most savage brutality. And to half-make a revolution is to dig your own grave.

But these things must be brought close to the experience of the audience. So, for the staging of *When Katherine Brewed,* adaptations can be permitted with agreement from us, using contemporary references to make the story relevant for today. And there are parts of the script where alterations can be made for the purpose of age-appropriateness for youth theatre and school productions.

Devising the Play

When Katherine Brewed is a 'devised' piece. There are various forms and methods of devising that have in common a collective, democratic ethos and approach. The final script, rather than springing from a single writer and/or director's imagination, is intended to be a synergy of workshop inputs, skill sets, and perspectives contributed by a number of talented creatives. To that end, diversity in all its forms (age, nationality, ethnicity, gender expression, sexuality, mental and physical ability), was for us a key criterion for participation. The result is a richer, less predictable, and more satisfying experience for all participants, including the audience.

Following discussions in 2018, supported by our good friend Professor Andy Lamas at the University of Pennsylvania and financed by a grant from the (now defunct) *Artists' International Development Fund* (AIDF) of the British Council, we travelled to Philadelphia to workshop the story with members of the *Applied Mechanics Theatre Collective*. From this arose a first script draft, shared and fed back upon by all participants, leading to a second, which was further workshopped at the Rose and Crown Theatre in London with new material incorporated, e.g. the Rotherhithe 'King on a boat' scene. This version was presented as a rehearsed reading to an audience at the London Marxism 2022 Festival, who gave verbal and written feedback. Incorporating this, the resulting third draft was similarly presented, leading to a fourth. Having gone through three rounds of workshopping, the script was rehearsed once more, and, in October 2023, it toured to three trade-union-sponsored venues: the Rose and Crown Theatre in Walthamstow; The Moot House in Harlow; and The Casa in Liverpool. The resulting 'final' version is the one you read here. This will itself be tested and adapted by the rigour and experience of full-scale production. We encourage feedback from our readers and audiences.

Here we take the opportunity to say 'Thank you' to the participants of the devising workshops.

Philadelphia workshop participants: Colin Leggo; Rebecca Wright (Applied Mechanics); M K Tuomanen (Applied Mechanics); and Theodora Rodine.

London rehearsed readings and workshops: Kimberley Capero; Isabella West; Seyi Ogunniyi; Olga Groves; Megan Bryony Gibbs; Michelle Pittoni; Esther Neslen; and John Allen.

October 2023 tour: Leon Topley; Ellis Jupiter; Bradley Scott; Natalie Stringer; and Isabella Hart.

Funding the Play

The nature of the funding that supports any theatre production is intrinsic to its values, its implicit political character, and its final meaning. Actors for example, unless it is an entirely amateur production, should be paid at union rates and allowances from the earliest phases of the project, as ours always were. To fund the creation and performing of *When Katherine Brewed*, our own positions as socialist activists, connected to trade union and community struggles, were vitally important.

The initial grant of £5,000 from the AIDF enabled us to launch the project. Important donations also came from the Liverpool Network Theatre (£1,500) and the US-based International Herbert Marcuse Association ($1,500), the latter giving their award for work:

> ... at the intersection of the arts and Marcuse's Great Refusal, as a consciousness-raising and labor education theater project in support of labor/community solidarity amidst the current wave of nationwide strikes by students and professors at universities and by workers in other industries across Britain.

We also provided early finance ourselves from our own personal funds (£1,500). But we then had to work hard for more than a year to raise the funds required for the October 2023 performances. These came from 30 donations (cash and in-kind) by trade union regions, branches, and local trades councils (£3,000). We launched a crowdfunding campaign endorsed by national trade union leaders and left-wing Labour MPs (£2,000). And of course we sold tickets for the performances (£3,000). Over the course of the six-year journey of *When Katherine Brewed*, we raised nearly £20,000.

Raising this money was hard work and very time consuming. But in this way, we not only gained funds, but we also generated interest in the project, and a working-class audience to boot. Starting with little but our own ideas and resources, winning small pockets of funding from trade unions and labour-friendly organisations, and aware of the modest contribution our work represents, we have shown that this model can work. Today, we note other important examples such as Banner Theatre and Townsend Theatre Productions that have won funding from a range of trade unions for their national tours of working-class historical theatre. We applaud the support provided by Unite the Union for the 2024 tour of the comedy musical *We're Not Going Back* about the 1984/85

British miners' strike, told from the perspective of three sisters who were part of the Women Against Pit Closures movement, by the Red Ladder Theatre Company. And we will add here the trade union support that has been forthcoming for the *Iron Ladies* film project, also about the 1984/85 British miners' strike, by Shut Out the Light productions.

Our Appeal

The purpose of the *When Katherine Brewed* theatre project was not one of comprehensive detail and exact re-enactment. This was never an exercise in historical investigation. Rather, we took the story of the rising of 1381 that emerged from those chronicles that were accessible to us, and from our reading of many of the various histories available today.

Neither of us are professional historians. We are socialists and enthusiasts of the movements for liberation that have gone before us. We do not seek simply to recreate the past, but to unite it with the present, and make it live for a current generation that fights for freedom today. That is what our four rebel characters are about: the intensity of the events they were caught up in; the previously unimaginable possibilities they were creating; the weaving together of historical and personal change; and the lessons of their experience for today.

In this period of ecological, economic, and political crisis, and the growth of the far right, it is more important than ever that the working class tells its own stories, not just in publications and lectures, but through the arts as well. As the final 2008 demise of the 7/84 theatre company sadly showed, mainstream funding is no longer a reliable nor even a likely means for making this happen, if it ever really was. However, we are optimistic that, with the support of the working-class movement, we will see the 'New Radical Theatre' of our own generation of struggle become increasingly well-known and influential, along with its democratic message of hope and resistance, inspired by the vision of a better, safer, and more equal world.

Mark and John
May 2025

When Katherine Brewed
A Play about the 1381 English Peasants' Revolt

Written by John Cresswell

Cast

- Mechanical 1 – Fool/John Ball
- Mechanical 2 – King Richard II – Elizabeth Tyler – They Stayed at Home – Joan
- Mechanical 3 – John Tyler – Wat Tyler – Katherine of Lakenheath – Archbishop Sudbury
- Mechanical 4 – William Walworth (Mayor of London) – Bartholomew Fletcher – King's official/Peasant/Tax collector 1
- Mechanical 5 – Lord Salisbury – Godwin Rolfe – King's official/Peasant/Tax collector 2
- Drummer – Eyewitness

When Katherine Brewed can be performed in a theatre; however, it has primarily been conceived as a low-cost project, easily staged in non-traditional spaces, indoor and out, using little or no stage technology. Character differentiation should be achieved mainly via physicality and voice. Costume and props should be 'signifiers' only, minimal, cheap and simple, e.g. Walworth's toy dagger. Some, but not all, of these are indicated in the script. The live percussionist/drummer plays throughout to create tension and atmosphere and to facilitate scene transitions, which should be slick and feel like an organic part of the performance.

Casting should prioritise diversity.
Running time is approximately 90 minutes with no interval.
Publicity should carry a trigger warning of references to violence, including sexual violence.

Scene 1

(*Four empty chairs upstage.* **Drummer** *onstage, quietly practising as audience enters. When audience is more or less settled,* **Drummer** *'signals' five modern day* **Mechanicals**; *e.g. Road Worker, Nurse, Barista, Cycle Courier, Postal Worker to begin 'arriving'. Nervous and excited, each will acknowledge audience in their own way and chat with each other. This tone, 'an amateur group of enthusiastic workers putting on a play', should be maintained throughout, particularly in transitions, with playful banter, helpfulness and mischief. Any 'mistakes', real or rehearsed, should be owned and enjoyed.* **Mechanical 1** *enters first bearing a large cycle delivery courier bag or similar. Inside are five supermarket carrier bags containing each* **Mechanical's** *simple costumes, props and signifiers.* **M1** *begins placing these at the appropriate empty chair.* **Sudbury's** *severed head prop, wearing a copy of his signifier, a bishop's mitre, should be left hidden in* **M1**'s *carrier.* **M2** *is next, and, once they have ordered their character's props and signifiers, will begin quietly and playfully practising a medieval song with* **Drummer**. *Meanwhile,* **M3** *and* **M4** *arrive and organise their costumes/props/character signifiers. This should be done so the audience can see, and be intrigued by, what these might indicate.* **M5** *is late with apologies to audience and other* **Ms**, *carrying the bag containing the placards, letters, etc. which need to be stored flat. The other* **Ms** *collect and order those that belong to them. Scene descriptor placards are placed onstage in order of use and so that the audience cannot read them.* **M5** *finds a string of plastic sausages in their bag.* **M1** *has been looking for these and takes them.* **M5** *and* **M4** *are puzzled.* **M1** *shows them the place in the script;* **M5** *and* **M4** *are disgusted, shrugging 'that's not funny'.* **M1** *tucks the sausages into one of their many pockets, then puts on* **Fool's** *signifier, becoming* **Fool**. *When all* **Ms** *are organised, indicating to* **Fool** *that this is so,* **Fool** *gives the message to audience to turn off phones, etc. Next* **Fool** *explains that 'When Adam delved and Eve span—who was then the gentleman?' would have been a commonly heard and understood peasant rebuttal to the 'divine right' of monarchs to rule.* **Fool** *then leads the audience in a practice call-and-response participation, which they will be encouraged to do whenever they hear the phrase during the play. After which,* **M4** *stands, drawing and flourishing the wooden spoon. Apologising to* audience, **Fool** *swaps the spoon for* **Walworth**'*s signifier, a toy jewelled dagger.* **M4** *draws again. At this,* **Fool** *silences* **M2***, encouraging* **M4** *to continue.* **Drummer** *continues. All watch* **M4**)

Mechanical 4

(*Reading a label on the dagger*) William Walworth, a prosperous merchant, now Mayor of London.

(*Moving centre stage,* **M4***, first practising the* **Wat Tyler** *killing thrust of Scene 25, with a few false starts and directed by* **Fool***, 'becomes'* **Walworth**)

Walworth

Richard. Alas, I carry bad … Your Majesty, there are ill tidings from … Lord Buckingham has returned, defeated, not defeated, *un*victorious from France. Meaning we cannot, *immediately*, afford further … Damnation, it will not do! (*Looks about him*) Where is that old fool …?

Mechanical 5

(*Has been studying the label on* **Lord Salisbury's** *signifier*) The aged and dignified statesman, Lord …

Walworth

Salisbury, there you are. Have you seen Richard?

(*Encouraged by* **Ms 2** *and* **3***, the nervous* **M5** *'becomes'* **Salisbury***. Indicating* **Ms 4** *and* **5** *should continue,* **Fool** *begins composing* **The Letter**)

Salisbury

Lord Salisbury and *King* Richard. He is fourteen now, Walworth, you really must get used to …

Walworth

Lord Mayor Walworth. (*Impatiently*) I have … *more* bad news.

Salisbury

(*Sighs*) Buckingham? (**Walworth** *nods*)

Walworth

Rich ... the King must be told.

Salisbury

He will not be pleased.

Walworth

When is he ever?

Salisbury

(*Drily*) I did it last time.

Walworth

(*Sighs*) That's why I am looking for him. Where is the little shi ..?

(**M2** *is trying on the* **King**'s *signifier, a cheap plastic crown, just as* **Salisbury** *and* **Walworth** *spot them. Throughout the play,* **Walworth** *will aim to be at* **King's** *left shoulder,* **Salisbury** *his right*)

Salisbury/Walworth

Your Majesty!

(*Alarmed,* **M2** *dashes back to their chair. Exasperated,* **Walworth** *and* **Salisbury** *follow.* **Fool** *takes the stage, carefully folding and putting away* **The Letter**. *Ever present,* **Fool** *will ad lib/joke according to each production's context, direct/play with the* **Mechanicals** *and react to the audience*)

Fool

(*To audience*) Good morrow, friends all! Court Fool here. Born to serve and amuse his Royal Highness, King Richard the Second. (*Turns to introduce* **King**, *but* **M2** *is puzzling over their script and still not wearing the crown*) He'll be here in a minute. Tricky age, fourteen, isn't it? Neither man nor boy. When I was fourteen all I wanted was a hat. He has one worth more than Kent, Essex and half the guilds in London. Got a temper too. *Never* look him in the eye is my advice. Last fellow who did ended with his head on a pike and his sweetmeats strung up across London Bridge. Messy.

(*Has a thought. Quickly changes something in* **The Letter**)

Before he comes then, set the scene, quick trot through how it works back in ye olde late fourteenth century England. 'The Serf (**Fool** *directs* **M3** *to become* **John Tyler** *frozen in work position upstage centre, handing him his signifier, a working tool.* **John Tyler** *will be a constant presence throughout this scene, at no point making eye contact with a Noble character.* **Fool** *will use* **M3/John Tyler** *as a prop and butt for jokes*) worked the land and the Lord (**Fool** *freezes into a Lord, ordering or abusing* **John Tyler**) worked the Serf!'[1] Pretty much it really. This one we'll call John Tyler, 'cos he's a Tiler, right? Or his grandfather was, before the great pestilence of 1347 took all but one of his brood.[2] Fat buboes bursting stinking pus all over, entire villages expiring in a day, writhing in terror, nobody left to bury the purulent corpses. After that, there were precious few houses left to tile. Just empty villages and untended fields, wastelands, famine, mass graves and weeping, weeping, shattered survivors.

(*Pause while* **Fool** *and* **John Tyler** *contemplate the utter horror of it all*)

Anyhoo, mustn't dwell. Besides, it wasn't all bad ... Tell a lie, it was *all* bad. Nearly everybody you knew or loved was suddenly dead in inexplicable agony for God's sake! (*Quickly adds to* **The Letter**) Meanwhile, half the population might have given up the ghost, but the Lord's belly was just as large, far fewer of them had died of course. But ... *if* you'd survived the 'Black Death'[3] and weren't so traumatised you went screaming mad, fewer serfs meant competition for scarce labour, equaled pressure on wages to go up plus an opportunity for the odd bondsman to scarper

---

1   The position of the serfs of England was wretched. However, there were differences by region. In Essex, serfdom (or villeinage) was still a dominant economic form, with peasants tied to the manor. However, in Kent, where trade with France had been developing throughout the century, 'the manor' was largely a thing of the past, and the 'peasantry' much more involved in trade and trade-related occupations.
2   There were many plagues and pestilences in this period.
3   The 'Black Death' was the phrase coined by the Elizabethan historian John Stow for the Bubonic Plague that swept through Europe in the middle of the 14th-century, claiming the lives of between a third and a half of the human population. It came into Britain at the port of Melcombe Regis on the Dorsetshire coast, 1348, carried by rats on merchant ships. The victims died horribly, in screaming pain, the lymphatic areas of the groin and armpits swollen with intensely painful 'ashy buboes'.

off to a more congenial Lord without a hue and cry landing them in the stocks.[4] By the late 1370s, thirty odd years of economic, biological and ecological crisis, not to mention disastrous foreign wars—am I ringing any bells here?—is producing cracks in the ancient feudal system of oppression and exploitation. Bringing us nicely to our John. Bit of a dreamer. Father of a sizeable brood himself.

King

(*Now crowned. On chair, reading script*) Fool!

Fool

(*With some urgency*) You are about to experience a *true* story. (*When a character is named the relevant* **M** *must jump into signifier/pose, remaining frozen until they need to change, except for* **M3** *who must keep returning to* **John Tyler**. *This should be fast and funny, especially as* **M3** *has to do it many times.* **Fool** *should enjoy 'playing' with the* **Ms** *in this way*) Archbishop of Canterbury Sudbury, Lord Salisbury and Mayor of London William Walworth *definitely* existed. Copies remain of the speech John Ball made at Blackheath on the 12th of June.

(**Mechanical 2** *produces* **John Ball's** *homemade wooden cross/ signifier, but no-one will accept it. Not knowing where to put it,* **M2** *tucks it into one of* **Fool's** *pockets*)

Ditto King Richard's speech to a delegation of the last Essex rebels. But ... using *exactly* those words? See, all our information comes from (*reverentially*) 'The Chronicles'. Some written around the time, others not. (*Significantly*) They don't all say the same thing. *None* of them was written by a Peasant.[5]

---

4   The labour shortage created by the plague advantaged the land serfs who could negotiate their terms with landowners, especially during the harvest. Attempts were made by the medieval state to regulate wages back to pre-plague levels with the Statute of Labourers, and even to regulate dress and ornament with the Sumptuary Laws.

5   There are many details of the Revolt that must be seen as to some degree speculative. The chronicles are not always consistent, and all were written with political agendas in one way or another. The numbers on the march, the exact whereabouts of key

King

(*Still frozen*) Fool!

Fool

(*More urgently*) One man was executed for disobeying Wat Tyler's orders not to loot. John Tyler—no relation, confusing, isn't it? — and his daughter Elizabeth sparked the Revolt. Thirty, not twenty or forty, thousand peasants marched on London.[6] Salisbury's biggest objection to them was their dress sense. (*Shrugs*) Some chronicles say so, others don't. Same with our title character, Katherine of Lakenheath. (*Exhausted*, **M3/Katherine** *should get into her 'one foot on the boat the other on the riverbank' pose of* Scene 11. **Fool** *laughs*) Did she *really* ...?

All Mechanicals

Fool!!

Fool

(*Flourishes a placard with the single word* **'Probably'** *to be used throughout the play. Encourages the audience to read it out*)

Alright. It's ... (*Licks and holds finger up to the wind*) February 1381 and ...

King[7]

(*Entering, full of pubescent righteousness*) Fool!

Fool

(*Pockets* **The Letter**. *Quick 'eyes front' to* **M3/John Tyler**) You'll see.

---

    protagonists at specific moments of the drama, the precise details of the various exchanges between the royal group and the rebels etc., are all matters of historical debate.

6   A measure of the significance of the march is that the entire population of London itself did not exceed 40,000.

7   King Richard II (1367–1400). Richard is described in several of the chronicles as a manipulated figure. The Oxford Dictionary of National Biography describes him as "Abrupt and stammering in speech, hasty and subject to sudden gusts of passion ..."

Scene 2

(*This scene should be fast paced and funny, occasionally veering, but not too far, into slapstick//panto villain/farce. The three noble characters are caricatures but based on real people taking decisions that had serious and bloody consequences*)

King

Amuse me.

Fool

Certainly, your Majesty. Have you heard the one about the Guildsman, the Flemish Weaver and the Gong dealer?

King

None of your incomprehensible lower-class stupidities.

Fool

(*Thinks*) John 'O' Gaunt[8] visits the apothecary to have his shrunken ...

King

And nothing disrespectful to my honoured Uncle. (*A smile is controlled*) Later perhaps.

Fool

As you wish, Sire. A song then. (*Quick discussion and agreement with* **Drummer** *who cues* **Fool** *up*)

King

(*As* **Fool** *is about to begin*) No! Look at me! (**Fool** *takes tiny, uncomfortable glances*) Properly! (**Fool** *tries again*) I want a war.[9]

---

8   John of Gaunt was the King's uncle, and an important figure in the politics of England at this time. He owned estates in all parts of the kingdom and had his own army. One of his properties was The Savoy in London, one of the most sumptuous palaces in Europe. Gaunt was seen by many (including Gaunt) as a rival for the throne.

9   England had been at war with France on and off since the middle of the century. Historians would later refer to this period as 'the Hundred Years War'. At this time, the wars were going badly for the English armies.

What's the point of being King otherwise?

Fool

(*To audience*) What indeed?

King

The King of France has as many as he likes.

Fool

He *will* keep winning them.

King

Don't speak. *Do* something funny. (*Stumped for a second,* **Fool** *prepares an elaborate physical trick involving the sausages and* **M3/JT**. *Just as it is about to start*) Salisbury says ... You may make fun of that senile old spoilsport.

Fool

With pleasure, Sire (*checks nervously around*). He isn't ..?

King

Just do it!

Fool

My Lord Salisbury ... (*Becoming a very doddery* **Salisbury** *on the toilet, using the sausages as painfully extruded piles.* **M3/JT** *stifles a laugh*) is so constipated that when he sits upon the privy, his ... nethers ...

King

(*Not amused*) The Peasants are not happy, he says.

Fool

(*Tucking the sausages away*) How can that possibly be, Sire?

King

(*Eyes* **Fool** *suspiciously*) Have a care, fool. I am not in the mood to be ...

(**Salisbury** *enters. Immediately* **King** *becomes several years younger.* **Salisbury** *does not like* **Fool** *being there.* **Fool** *will constantly 'play with fire', hiding behind* **King's** *power whilst undermining and ridiculing* **Salisbury** *and* **Walworth**)

Salisbury

There you are, Richard.

King

(*Sulky and resentful*) King Richard. Or your Majesty.

Salisbury

(*Nods deferentially*) Of course.

King

Say it then!

Salisbury

Your *Majesty* ... must stop running away whenever 'difficult' matters arise.

King

(*Almost in tears*) I did not run away! I was merely ...

(**Walworth** *arrives, practising the killing thrust on* **M3/JT**. *Glares suspiciously at* **Fool**)

Walworth. (**Salisbury** *ahems. Resentfully*) Mayor of London Walworth. Even you deny me.

Walworth

(*Not happy to be in agreement with* **Salisbury**) Rich ... (**Salisbury** *'ahems' again*) Your *Highness*, regretfully, at this moment, I must concur with Salis ... *Lord* Salisbury. Continuing the war simply isn't possible.

King

(*To* **Salisbury**, *thoughtfully*) Because the Peasants are not happy.

Salisbury

(*Surprised* **King** *has been paying attention*) I am gratified his Majesty has attended so closely to our argument.

King

Oh, always, my honoured Lords. (*With exaggerated sincerity*) Every word imparted upon our unworldly ears by counsel older and wiser is treasure beyond value. (**Salisbury** *and* **Walworth** *are pleased* **King** *is addressing them respectfully for once. Knowing better,* **Fool** *winks 'wait for it' at the audience and* **M3/JT**) The Peasants suffer, you advise me. (**King** *'sad faces'* **M3/JT**) I trust and believe you, having but one question. (*Deeply considering it.* **Salisbury** *and* **Walworth** *lean closer*) So fucking what!? (**Fool** *'I told you so's' the audience and* **M3/JT**) Peasants are born to suffer, Kings to make war. So it has been, so it is, so it always shall be. (*Challenging*) Is this not what you, with great pains have taught me, Lord Salisbury?

Salisbury

(*Sharing his despair with* **Walworth**. *Deferentially*) Indeed, your Majesty, but in this *particular* case ...

King

If it were the army, I could understand, but *they* could not be in greater spirits. Several soldiers told me so last week, on their deathbeds. (to **Fool**) To die for one's King is the greatest honour.

Fool

(*To audience*) There has been a great deal of 'honour' recently.

Salisbury

(*Patiently, sensing an opportunity*) His Majesty shows great wisdom in raising the condition and morale of the army. They pertain greatly to the matter in hand.

King

(*Not understanding and suspicious of the flattery*) How?

Walworth

(**Salisbury** *signals this is the moment*) It appears the brave and honourable Lord Buckingham ... glorious and worthy of heroic ballad though his expedition to France undoubtedly was ... (**Salisbury** *'ahems'* **Walworth** *to get on with it*) was *not*, as hoped, *completely* triumphant.[10]

Fool

(*Leaping forward*) Presenting for your noble pleasures. 'Lord Buckingham's glorious and heroic, *not* completely triumphant expedition to France!'

(*To dramatic drumming,* **Fool** *performs in still images; standing firm—looking worried—very scared—soiling himself—running with sticky underwear—begging for mercy.* **M3/JT** *desperately stopping themselves from laughing. At first,* **King** *is highly amused, then notices* **Salisbury** *and* **Walworth's** *growing discomfort*)

King

(*Confronting them*) This is a true account? (*Highly embarrassed, they do not deny it*). (*Furious*) Then I... *England* must be avenged!

Salisbury

(*Honour stung*) Do not doubt it, Majesty.

King

Immediately!

Walworth

Our *most* ardent desire, Sire. But to continue the wars we *first* must have more supplies, weapons and soldiers. (**Walworth** *looks desperately to* **Salisbury**)

Salisbury

(*As if to a young child*) The Peasants *grow* the food, which *feeds* the horses and soldiery, also the blacksmiths and artisans who *craft*

---

10   Buckingham's army had been soundly beaten in France, and what was left of it had returned and was now camped in Wales.

the weapons, ships and carts. Peasants *are* the soldiers. Their taxes *pay* for all.[11]

King

(*To* **Fool**) Is it any wonder these two are not King? So get the Peasants to grow *more* food, become *more* soldiers. Make every adult in the land pay *more* tax.

Salisbury

(*Hurriedly*) Except the nobility, Sire?

King

Obviously.

Walworth

(*Sarcastic*) And the Church of course.[12]

King

(*Impatiently*) Every *other* adult in the country. Over fourteen. Call it ... a 'Poll' tax.

(**M3/JT** *alarmed.* **Fool** *'Wait, see where I'm going with this.'* **King** *is delighted with his idea, which* **Salisbury** *and* **Walworth** *must stop, neither wanting to be the one*)

Salisbury

(*Losing the contest*) It is one thing to *say* you are going to tax the Peasantry. *Collecting* it when in the countryside the knife of hunger glints honed and sharp ... (**King/JT** *don't understand.* **Fool** *suggests* **Salisbury** *try again more simply*) When such fat as there was is long since pared ... (**King/JT** *still lost.* **Fool** *'Nope's!'* **Salisbury**) Because we have taken so much already and they are starving, is another matter. (**King/JT** *finally get it.* **Fool** *'congratulates'* **Salisbury**)

---

11   The English wars in France had drained the national coffers and the population had already suffered two poll taxes to pay for them.
12   The church in this period owned its own estates. The papacy in Rome could also levy taxes via the English church, a major annoyance to the Royal court.

King

(*Not ready to give up his perfect idea*) Tell them it's for a war.

Walworth

(*Almost losing his patience*) It's *always* for a war.

(*Is light dawning? No. Exasperation all around*)

Fool

(*To* **Walworth/Salisbury**) With your permissions?

(*They are suspicious but out of ideas.* **Fool** *takes the stage, directing* **M3/JT** *to become a 'throne'.* **King** *is sat upon it*)

His magnificence recalls the apple seedlings his Father planted in the royal garden?

King

(*After a moment's thought*) I wanted fresh ones always at hand.

Fool

Why should you not? You were a Prince. And what a shining epitome of …

Walworth

Get on with it, *fool*!

(*In revenge,* **Fool** *'encourages'* **Walworth** *and* **Salisbury** *to 'become' the apple seedlings. Reluctantly they do, growing strongly.* **King** *is highly amused*)

Fool

The seedlings sprouted and grew.

King

(*Remembering*) I wanted them in my bedchamber where I could look after them. (*Fiercely*) That ass of a gardener told me I shouldn't.

Fool

    Only once, Sire. (**M3/JT** *sticks out tongue which* **Fool** *slices off*) And then ..?

King

    They (*frowns*) ... What have apples got to do with me having a war?

Fool

    The saplings, your Majesty. In your dry, *dark* bedchamber. They became ..?

King

    (*Under breath, like a told off child*) Withered and brown.

Fool

    (*Cocks an ear*) Your Majesty?

King

    (*Loudly*) Withered and brown.

Fool

    (*'Directing'* **Walworth** *and* **Salisbury** *to wither*) And then?

King

    There were no apples. I was ... very sad.

Fool

    We remember it so.

    (*'Allows'* **Walworth** *and* **Salisbury** *to become themselves. Rubbing his back,* **M3/JT** *resumes the working freeze*)

    (*Gently*) It is the same with Peasants, your Majesty. If you deny *them* the means to survive, they too will be *un*able to provide you with the things *you* need.

King

(*Thoughtfully*) I *have* often wondered why Peasants look so withered and brown.

(**M3/JT** *rolls their eyes.* **Fool, Salisbury** *and* **Walworth** *wait in suspense. They have all tried. Has* **King** *actually got it this time? No. He has another 'brilliant' idea*)

What about the Archbishop of Canterbury?

Salisbury

(*Panicked look to* **Walworth**) I hardly think we need bring Lord Sudbury into …

King

He's the nearest to God after me. Or is it I'm after him? (*Nobody is sure*) Anyway, get *Sudbury* to tell the priests to tell the Peasants that if they don't pay more tax, they will all go to Hell. That usually works, doesn't it? Where is Sudbury anyway? Shouldn't he be here? (*Calling offstage*) Bring me Sudbury.

(**M3/JT** *points to themself 'that's me, isn't it?'* **Fool** *shakes head, 'not yet.'*)

(*Noticing the expressions on the Nobles' faces*) What?

Walworth

(*Sceptically*) A hundred years ago, even in your grandfather's time perhaps … (*looks to* **Salisbury**)

Salisbury

(*Very uncomfortable*) *Now* the people do not entirely trust what they hear from the pulpit is the *actual* word of God.[13]

King

(*Genuinely interested*) Really? What do they hear?

---

13 The church was now split between a papacy in Rome and another at Avignon. Many were sceptical that the teachings of the 'official' church were really to be believed as the 'Word of God'.

Walworth

(*Cynically*) The truth.

King

Remind me.

(*It's story time again.* **Fool** *'encourages' a weary* **M3/JT** *to resume being the throne, then sits beside the* **King**, *mockingly attentive*)

Salisbury

(*Embarrassed, but this is the 'official' line*) Peasants, *all* people of a lower station, (*looking archly at* **Walworth** *who, as a merchant, is technically of 'lower station'*) are the sons and daughters of Adam's son Cain, the murderous dog who slew his brother and whose descendants are thus cursed for eternity.[14] Whilst we ...

King

Whilst we what?

Walworth

(*Sarcastically*) Are drawn from the line of Adam's obedient and civilised son, Seth.

King

I see. (*He doesn't. Back to audience, begins urinating on* **M3/JT**. *All scramble to avoid seeing the Royal penis*)

Fool

(*Happily*) Which explains, Sire, why churchmen and nobility do no work, wear silk clothes, own palaces, dine on the finest food and plenty of it. Why you in particular are the very pinnacle of culture, sophistication and civilised behaviour.

King

(*Scratches backside. Over his shoulder, still urinating*)

And my Peasants no longer believe this?

---

14   The phrase 'The children of Cain' expressed the sinful nature of humankind, forever in need of forgiveness.

Fool

(*To audience*) Incredible isn't it?

Walworth

(*Unable to contain himself*) Because most priests, Lord Sudbury in particular, are grasping, corrupt, venal liars.

Salisbury

(*Hissing.* **King** *should not be hearing this*) Not *all* priests are so.

Walworth

Pox-drenched whores have more chance of entering heaven than Sudbury.

Fool

(*To audience, indicating* **Walworth**) He would know.

Walworth

Where *is* the dog?

Fool

(*Aside, to* **Walworth**) At one of your 'establishments', your Mayorship?

King

(*Finished, putting himself away. With an aggrieved look at* **Fool**, **M3/JT** *returns to work pose*) Establishments?

Salisbury

(*Quickly*) There is one priest in particular, John Ball. (**M3/JT** *points 'isn't that you?' at a 'shushing'* **Fool**) Fortunately now in Sudbury's Maidstone jail.[15]

---

15 John Ball was currently imprisoned at Sudbury's Maidstone gaol. His release, followed by the conference at Maidstone with Wat Tyler, leader of the rebels, is one of the important turning points in the rising.

Walworth

Scum! I would tear his guts with my own teeth. (*Mimes more killing thrusts on the unreactive* **M3/JT**)

Salisbury

(*In his more refined way, also getting carried away*) He and his 'hedgerow' priests prey on congregations as they leave church, leading them to some hillside or field where they rant despicable heresy of a world where every man and woman is free and equal, no lords and vassals.[16] No ... Kings!

(*Entertained,* **King** *is caught between increasingly incensed advisors*)[17]

Walworth

Chew on his still beating heart, drink his hot blood ...

Salisbury

If Ball and his ilk had their way there would be no castles, no fine tapestries, no cultured and learned men ...

Walworth

... Bugger him with a longsword till his fucking eyes pop, tear his ballocks away with these hands and shove them up his stinking ... (*Becomes aware* **King** *is staring*)

Salisbury

as .... (*Noticing* **King** *too then the practically frothing* **Walworth**. *Weakly*) ... we.

King

(*While* **Walworth** *and* **Salisbury** *collect themselves. Dismissively*) Kill him. End his heresies.

(**M3/JT** *glances at* **Fool** *who tries to look busy*)

---

16 John Ball was known to wait for parishioners to come out of morning mass, to then preach his own message of opposition to the power and wealth of the Church.

17 The drama between these characters as shown here is told in the chronicle by Froissart, with Walworth as the hot-head and Salisbury as the wise counsellor in the group.

Salisbury

(*Uneasily*) To do such a thing to an *ordained* priest might be seen as ... permission. There are other members of the clergy for whom the people have *less* love.

Walworth

Where *is* that dog, Sudbury?

(**M3/JT** *points to themself again.* **Fool** *shakes head*)

Salisbury

Ball has a considerable, I cannot imagine why, *following* amongst the more gullible. They listen to him. His *ideas* are popular.

Walworth

Too damn popular!

King

Then kill all that listen to him. Wipe every single Peasant out if you have to. Until they believe what we tell them and pay what I need for a war.

(**Salisbury** *and* **Walworth** *are back to square one*)

Fool

(*With a nod to* **Drummer**) A revel, my masters! Of the King of France and an ague he picked up from a milkmaid's ...

King

I have it! Tell the Peasants they have *The King's* word. He needs one more war, which, if *all* of them pay *all* of the tax, we *will* win. After that, they need pay no ... *fewer* taxes because we will have all of France's money. They may not trust the Nobles or the Church, but they *do* trust *me*. (*To the audience, archly*) Everybody can trust the King.

(*This actually is a good idea. Besides,* **Walworth** *and* **Salisbury** *are exhausted*)

Walworth

It *might* work, Salisbury?

King

(*An excited child*) And *then* I can have my war?

Salisbury

(*Sighs*) As you wish, your Majesty.

(**King** *leaves happy, barking 'move!' at* **Fool** *who jumps aside, hiding behind* **M3/JT** *now their 'protection' is gone.* **Salisbury** *remains concerned*)

Even so, I doubt it will end well. The Peasants …

Walworth

(*Dismissing fears he has himself*) You worry too much, old man. (*Sneering at* **M3/JT**) What can a bunch of horse dumb, half-starved, leaderless serfs do?

Salisbury

(*Conversationally*) There is an estate near Agincourt, fertile land, a fine castle.

Walworth

Who does it belong to?

Salisbury

Me, soon.

Walworth

(*Laughs*) After all, the damn Frenchies can't keep beating us forever.

(**Walworth** *and* **Salisbury** *exit, also happier.* **Fool** *tucks* **The Letter** *in* **John Tyler's** *pocket*)

Fool

(*To audience*) What, as they say, can possibly go wrong?

(*Glancing down at* **The Letter, John Tyler** *returns, sternly frozen, into work position*)

Scene 3

Fool

(*Reads* **Scene 3** *descriptor placard then parades it across the stage to be placed, clearly visible for the duration of the scene. Subsequent scene descriptor placards follow the same procedure to be placed in front of the previous one. If projected, they are read out then remain until replaced by the next*)

Placard: 'March 1381: King Richard's Third Poll Tax Begins.'

(**Fool** *observes.* **John Tyler** *looks straight ahead*)

Tax collector 1

(*Enters, counting money*) This from seven villages. Isn't near enough.

(**Tax collector 2** *enters, shaking head in disbelief*)

How much this time?

Tax collector 2

Three groats![18]

Tax collector 1

Each family!? Impossible.

Tax collector 2

Each *person* over the age of fourteen, by May.

Tax collector 1

(*Incredulous*) Can't be done.

Tax collector 2

Then Hobb the Robber[19] will skin us live and tan our hides for leather.

---

18   Three groats was three times the amount levied in 1379. For villages across England, this tax was the final straw. The first sign of resistance was the 'disappearance' of huge numbers of people from their villages who could not or would not pay.

19   Hobb the Robber was the popular nickname given to Robert Hales, the King's treasurer. He was held responsible for the burden of taxation put upon the general

Tax collector 1

Aye. Then sell 'em back to us and still expect his money.

Tax collector 2

Gravediggers will have great employment this winter.

Tax collector 1

(*Thinking*) How will we know they're fourteen?

(**T/C 2** *points to their own armpit.* **T/C 1** *doesn't understand.* **T/C 2** *mimes plucking a genital pubic hair. A suggestive grin spreads across* **T/C 1's** *face*)[20]

I'm going to enjoy this!

(*They exit,* **T/C 1** *rubbing their hands with pleasure*)

Scene 4

Fool

Placard: '30th of May 1381: Village of Fobbing, Essex.'[21]

(**John Tyler** *works in time with drumming.* **Elizabeth** *works downstage.* **Tax collectors** *enter seeking 'customers'.* **T/C 1** *draws* **T/C 2's** *attention to* **Elizabeth***. Appraising her, they aren't sure.* **T/C 2** *approaches, checks round, not seeing* **John Tyler***, then whispers in her ear*)

Elizabeth

(*Offended*) Er, no!

(**Elizabeth** *resumes work.* **T/C 2** *returns, shrugging to* **T/C 1** *who shakes their head and approaches* **Elizabeth** *in the same way as* **T/C2**)

I said no!

---

population. He was another figure who was especially hated by many.

20 The pubic region was examined as a measure of age. This insult to the person and to the village was a major cause of antagonism and hatred directed towards the poll tax collectors.

21 The Essex village of Fobbing appears in the chronicle by Froissart as the village where the Revolt began.

(**T/C 1** *beckons* **T/C2** *over and together they try to lift her skirt. In the struggle,* **Elizabeth** *knees* **T/C1** *in the groin and escapes towards her father, pursued by a limping* **T/C 1** *and* **2** *who catches* **Elizabeth** *from behind*)

Father!

(**John Tyler** *stops working*)

Tax collector 2

(*Enjoying their work*) In the name of Sir Robert Hales, Lord Treasurer of England ...

Elizabeth

FATHER!

Tax collector 1

(*Kneeling in front of* **Elizabeth**. *Vengefully*) Hobb the Robber says show us your ...

(*As* **T/C1** *yanks up* **Elizabeth**'s *skirt, to a final bang on the drum* **John Tyler** *smashes the brains from* **T/C 1**)

John Tyler

Enough!

(*A stunned moment, before drumming restarts at pace.* **Tax collectors** *become* **Peasants**. *Horror/confusion becomes delight/understanding of the seriousness and implications. Remembering,* **John Tyler** *takes out* **The Letter**.[22] *Nobody can read and* **Fool** *has it thrust back into their hand. With 'apologies' to audience and 'The sooner you lot learn to read the better' to the* **Peasants, Fool** *reads*)

---

22 These letters were a form of communication and planning found on rebels who were arrested and executed after the rising had been suppressed. They were written cryptically in allegorical style in the manner of coded messages for those 'in the know' to interpret and understand.

Fool

> John Shep, sometime
> St Mary priest of York
> And now in Colchester.[23]
>
> (*Confusion, especially* **Elizabeth**)

John Tyler

> This is from John Ball.
>
> (*General understanding/pleasure/impressed*)

Fool

> Greeteth well John Nameless,
> And John Miller and John Carter.
>
> (*Confusion, especially* **Elizabeth**)

Peasant 1

> (*Indicating them all*) Us!
>
> (*General understanding/pleasure/impressed*)

Fool

> Biddeth Piers Plowman.[24]

Peasant 2

> That's you, John.
>
> (*Pleasure/embarrassment from* **John Tyler**)

Fool

> To go to his work and
> Chastise well Hobb the Robber.

---

23 John Ball's parish is thought to have been at Colchester.
24 Piers Plowman is the Christ-like figure, pure of heart, who is the central character in William Langland's epic poem of that name.

John Tyler

Chastise?

(*Shrugs from all*)

Elizabeth

(*With relish*) Chop his fucking head off!

(*Hand to mouth at what she has said. Cheers of agreement*)

Fool

(*Freezing actors. To audience, with urgency*) From one village in deepest Essex to thirty thousand storming London in a fortnight? How could the Revolt spread so fast and deep? Shake a bottle of bubbly and it will blow its cork, but it's time and work fermenting the fizz. Police horses charging peaceful protesters will provoke a riot to bring down 'The Iron Lady'. Without organisation, putting an angry quarter of a million on the streets there's nobody to gallop at. In other words, real spontaneity takes careful planning. Take this hilltop beacon Johnny T and his village are about to set alight.[25] (**Fool** *directs* **Ms** *to make it*) *Previously* constructed, kept ready and dry, hundreds like it the length and breadth. Think WhatsApp is fast? The peasants' call to arms flamed at the speed of light. Letters and a thousand 'hedgerow' sermons; John Ball and his renegade priests had sown a soil made fertile by half a hundred years of ruling class manure. When the tinder was lit, the people were ready. Thirty thousand in two weeks! (*Patting a determined* **John Tyler** *on the back*) Not bad for a bunch of horse dumb, half-starved, leaderless serfs![26]

---

25 The lighting of hilltop fires to spread news of the rising is mentioned in the *Anonomalle Chronicle*.

26 There is evidence of planning for the rising. In this period, there would be 'rumours' of things afoot, in anticipation of events. The Magna Societas is thought to have been the conspiratorial body, with Wat Tyler at its centre, that organised and carried out the release of John Ball, the taking of Rochester Castle, the march to Canterbury, and the march to and occupation of London, as well as the Mile End and Smithfield demands.

Scene 5

(**Fool** *brings* **Ms** *back to life. These next scenes at pace and slickly changed*)

Fool

Placard: 'Word Spreads Rapidly Through Hilltop Beacons.'

John Tyler

What are you waiting for? Light it.

(**Peasant 2** *lights the village beacon, watching it catch*)

Peasant 1

Do they see us? (*All gaze towards the next high point.* **Fool** *switches* **M5's** *head in the right direction*)

Elizabeth

Theirs is lit. (**Elizabeth** *takes on her signifier/pose*)

Fool

(*Compere of a boxing bout/talent show*) Introducing our first 'Campfire Comrade'. Historical figure (*uses 'Probably' placard*) with plausible claim for sparking the 1381 English Peasants revolt. Put your hands together for ... Elizabeth Tyler!

Scene 6

Fool

Placard: 'First Week of June: The Rebels Arm Themselves.'[27]

(*In awe,* **John Tyler**, **Elizabeth** *and* **Peasant 2** *enter an armoury. The weapons are heavy and unfamiliar.* **Bartholomew Fletcher**, *an ex-soldier, takes charge, handing a dagger to* **Elizabeth**, *demonstrating how to stab between armour joints.* **Peasant 2** *has the wooden spoon this time which* **Bartholomew** *replaces with a sword, modelling how*

---

27 The rebels broke into the armouries of the manor houses they stormed and armed themselves. Many ex-soldiers had also returned from France with their weapons to keep at home, their right under the Law of Winchester.

to wield it correctly. **John Tyler** *rejects a new weapon; his sharpened tool has served well so far.* **Drummer** *and* **Fool** *'mark the moment' as* **Bartholomew** *'discovers' a longbow*)

Bartholomew

Well met, old friend.

(*Bow raised,* **Bartholomew** *holds the pose*)

Fool

(*To audience*) Based firmly on historical research, we made our second Campfire Comrade up. Once longbowman of Edward III. Now fighting for justice, 'King Richard and the True Commons'. Please welcome, Bartholomew Fletcher!

Scene 7

Fool

Placard: '6th of June: Rochester Castle Taken.[28] Ruling Power Crumbles.'

(**Godwin Rolfe**; *a prisoner in his cell, sits hopelessly awaiting execution. His signifier is a lipstick painted* 'F' *for Felon on his cheek. This must be scrubbed and re-applied each time* **M5** *changes role.* **Bartholomew, John Tyler** *and* **Elizabeth** *burst in*)

Godwin

Is it time already?

Bartholomew

There'll be no execution today, friend. Not of you anyway.

(**Elizabeth** *gently raises him to his feet*)

---

28 Rochester Castle was one of the strongest fortifications in England. Positioned on the Medway in anticipation of a French invasion, it was a symbol of Norman military prowess. Its falling to the Rebels was the first sign to the Royal Court that the rising was unlike the small local skirmishes that occurred from time to time. This was a movement that threatened their political power and social control.

Elizabeth

You're free!

Godwin

Thank God!

John Tyler

Thank Wat Tyler!

(*The three move on to other cells. Breathing free air,* **Godwin** *takes his pose*)

Fool

Another well-sourced invention—condemned prisoner of (**Godwin** *spits*) Archbishop Sudbury and third Campfire comrade. Give it up folks for ... Godwin Rolfe!

Scene 8

Fool

Placard: '7th of June: 20,000 Peasants Free John Ball from Maidstone Gaol.'[29]

Katherine

(*To audience/prison guards*) Who's asking? Katherine of Lakenheath that's who. (*Proudly*) Widow and brewer and it would suit you well to open this gate to my peaceful request before ...

(*The well-armed* **Elizabeth, Bartholomew** *and* **Godwin** *arrive*)

You took your time.

Bartholomew

John Ball? Is he within?

Katherine

Many poor souls beside.

---

29 The liberation of the prisoners of the Maidstone prison, along with John Ball, was another significant moment in the early phase of the Revolt.

Godwin

(*With venom*) And Sudbury?

Katherine

(*Scornfully*) Our fine Archbishop has fled to London hoping to hide from justice.

Godwin

He will not.

Bartholomew

Inside. Free John Ball.

(**Godwin** *and* **Elizabeth** *leave*)

Katherine

(*To* **Bartholomew**) See that *brave* prison guard now running for his skin. I once saw him spit on Ball's food.

(**Bartholomew** *fires an arrow.* **Fool** *mimes getting hit in the eye.* 'Sorry, wrong story!' *then* 'Arrgh!')

(*Calling after the guard*) I warned you! (*Takes her pose*)

Fool

Last, but definitely not least, fourth Campfire Comrade, genuine, verifiable (*'Probably' placard*) participant in this evening's momentous and extraordinary historical events. Shout it out for our title character: widow, brewer and rebel, Katherine of Lakenheath!

Scene 9

Fool

Placard: '10th/11th of June 1381: Children of Cain on the Road to London.'

(**Drummer** *steps forward, a military beat*)

Elizabeth

One, two, three, four, five, six, seven, (**Godwin** *enters*) eight, nine ...

Godwin/Elizabeth

Ten, twenty, thirty, forty, fifty, sixty, seventy, eighty, (**Katherine** *enters*) ninety ...

Katherine/Elizabeth/Godwin

One hundred, two hundred, three hundred, four hundred, five hundred, six hundred, seven hundred, eight hundred (**Bartholomew** *enters*), nine hundred ...

Bartholomew/Katherine/Elizabeth/Godwin

One thousand, two thousand, three thousand, four thousand, five thousand, six thousand, seven thousand, eight thousand, nine thousand, ten thousand, (*louder*), twenty thousand, thirty thousand. Thirty thousand gathered. Thirty thousand gathered.[30]

Elizabeth

And we marched!

(*Led by* **Drummer**, *all exit triumphantly*)

Scene 10

Fool

Placard: 'They Stayed at Home.'

They Stayed at Home

(*Working, raises eyes to the audience, defiant*)

There were animals to tend. And Mother, who would have died. Who did die, a week after everybody had left. Buried her as

---

[30] The chronicle by Froissart suggests two rebel armies, one from Essex under the leadership of Jack Straw, the other from Kent under the leadership of Wat Tyler, of 30,000 each. Whatever the true figure, we can be sure that these were huge gatherings for the time, and that in total they were significantly greater in number than the London population.

decently as I could without the priest. Looked out that night, beacons calling more, like Jesus' star. Next day, I milked our goat and others that strayed, moaning, to our door. Patched a hole in the neighbour's roof. When it rained, no drop got in. I never left the village. Still haven't. Near a week I didn't speak to a single person. So strange. So peaceful. Did as much work as needed then sat, watching and listening, thinking. What *was* God's will in this? Then they began to return. Not all. Such stories. Manors sacked. Great palaces burned! Nobles and lords executed! The king! Freedom given then taken back! I was glad to see them, but the noise they made and some were different. Few thanks I got though goodness knows what they'd have done had their beasts died. Another week and the lord's men came back too, looking for those had changed the most. An old spinster the village had spurned and mocked, who had spoken loudest, shaming strong men to go, was taken. Facing tortures and a death to quail martyrs, she would not deny 'Good John Ball' or 'Brave Wat Tyler'.

Didn't know who they were then.

I do now.

Scene 11

Fool

Placard: '12th June, Blackheath: Peasant Army Camp, One Day from London.'[31]

(**Campfire Comrades** *sit around their fire—one of a thousand—thrilled/disbelieving that they should be here this day, talking, debating, sharing tales of what they have done and seen, their plans and hopes. A burst of laughter as we join them. All are hugely enjoying* **Katherine** *telling her story. But there is pain behind the joy*)

---

31 On the night of the 12th of June, the Kent army camped at Blackheath, outside the walls of London. The next day was the feast of Corpus Christie when John Ball would make his historic speech at dawn, before the occupation of London.

Katherine

... 'Let me on that boat, Crone!' roars my master, the fat ball of dripping pig's grease. 'Can't you see they mean to murder me?' He spoke true, the village *was* fast behind, tools sharpened for the job. 'If you can speak my name,' says I, one foot on the boat planks, the other on the shore. 'If you can speak my name.' (*Takes this pose.* **Fool** *hands her the wooden spoon, she wields it as a weapon*) Course he couldn't. One villein is all the same as another to a ... (*interrupted by* **Fool** *as someone arguing* **Salisbury's** *origin story at another campfire*) So says your pulpit priest Sunday when you have scarce the strength to listen. But Cain and his brothers were *not* the first to walk God's Earth. (**Elizabeth** *is hearing this for the first time; the others have before but are happy to again in these circumstances*) Before them were Adam and Eve, living sinless in Paradise. (*Loudly*) In that Eden were neither rich nor poor, lords and ladies in their manors, nor serfs in their hovels treated worse than swine. No 'pious' bishops on their soft, fat arses, milking us dry. Only honest working folk. How it was in God's *true* beginning is how it should be now and forever. (*Making her point*) *No* sin to wish it, *none* to make it be.

Bartholomew

(*Happy in agreement*) So says good John Ball, and I for one believe him. (*Calling*) 'When Adam delved and Eve span—'

All except Elizabeth

(*Responding*) '—Who was then the gentleman!?'

(**Fool** *encourages the audience to join, getting the comrades to repeat, in role, if necessary. Laughter, agreement, pleasure. Still standing,* **Bartholomew** *summons courage to tell his story*)

Elizabeth

(*Before he can, to* **Katherine**, *who has sat next to her, a bond between them already formed*) So, what happened? Did you let your lord on the boat? Did he escape?

Katherine

Hmm? Oh! (*Returning to her previous stance. Somewhat relieved,* **Bartholomew** *sits*) Next, he fumbles for his dagger, which his fear-slicked fingers let fall in the mud. 'Katherine,' I tells him fast, there weren't much time for waiting, 'of Lakenheath. Widow and brewer, *independent* woman. Made so by you if you would but remember.' 'Gold!' cries he, scrabbling in his bulging purse. 'Now for pity's sake let me ...'

Godwin

Gold!? How much?

Katherine

(*Tutting him quiet, this is a serious part*) 'When my Thomas died,' I reminds him, 'leg smashed by one of your men's carts, though we begged, you would not stop the church taking our only milker.'

Elizabeth

Mortuary they call that tax, when the head of a family passes. Our friary has a fine herd thanks to it.

Katherine

Death it was to my newborn grandson whose mother died bearing him.

(*Uncomfortable pause. Assuming the story is over,* **Bartholomew** *prepares again to speak*)

Godwin

(*Joking, but all too familiar with suffering and the death of family*) You were talking of gold. (**Bartholomew** *sits again*) You have it?

Katherine

Gave it to the ferryman in payment for his boat I cast adrift, with one small kick. (*Miming this, with grim satisfaction she watches it drift away*) Wouldn't take it though. We threw it together into the pit scraped for our once fine master. (*To* **Bartholomew**, *shaking away the darkness*) You've seen him? Good John Ball.

Godwin

(*Before **Bartholomew** can admit he hasn't*) Shared a cell with him for a time. (*Immediately has the floor. Embarrassed to be the centre of attention*) Never complained, not Ball. Spoke as you've been, but soft. His words had power, no need to rage. After a while, even the warders would do him no harm. Drove my lord archbishop wild that did.

Katherine

Sudbury?

Godwin

(*Spits*) Would've drawn the poor priest's guts hisself, but feared dirtying his precious ermine robes.

Elizabeth

(*Nervously blurted*) Why were you in prison?

Katherine

(*Half-joking, slowly stirring the stew*) Could use some meat. A rapist's ballocks would do.

(**Elizabeth** *giggles.* **Bartholomew** *finds something of great interest in his bow*)

Godwin

(*Angrily, showing the **F** on his cheek*) Thief's what I am! Leave the raping to Hobb the Robber's men. Honest serf I was. Church land we rented though little comfort they gave when the pestilence took my wife, three lads and the little one. (*Any remaining smiles disappear*) Same tithes due they said, but how was I to till my plots with none but a lame old father to help? When he died too, I couldn't pay Heriot[32] due, so they threw me off. It was starve or steal. I chose to live, that one day I might confide to our great archbishop my 'thoughts' on his holy office. A week ago that was a condemned man's dream. Now, maybe, I might. (*to* **Katherine**)

---

32 Heriot: effectively a death duty, requiring the serf to give up their 'best beast' to the lord.

Put that in your stew, you old ..!

Bartholomew

Peace! (*Stands between* **Godwin** *and* **Katherine**. *Importantly*) Poverty will make harlots of the saints. (*Agreement, grudging from* **Katherine**. *In the meantime, summoning courage again*) I myself have ...

Elizabeth

(*Looking around in excitement and wonder*) So many people. They say we are going to London. What will we do when we get there?

Bartholomew

(*With relief, but somewhat pompous, to the amusement of the others who nonetheless listen with respect, as does* **Fool**) Speak with the king. The boy *cannot* know what's done in his name. (*The others are not so certain*)

Katherine

(*Gently ribbing*) You hold that bow like an old lover. You were an archer?

Bartholomew

(*Finally, but now not so sure he wants to*) Five years in France I served. Hundreds here the same. (*Standing to attention*) Fought for the Black Prince when we took Limoges.[33] (**Fool** *has* **Drummer** *launch into a military beat, leading* **Bartholomew**, *despite himself, around the stage, both losing themselves in the memory of parading victorious into Limoges. Caught in the moment,* **Godwin**, *then* **Katherine** *joins behind.* **Elizabeth**, *tending the stew, enjoys the performance. Approaching her,* **Drummer** *falters and halts.* **Drummer** *and* **Bartholomew** *stare at* **Elizabeth**, *then, having difficulty meeting each other's gaze, each other*) Wicked and shameful deeds were done that day to thousands

---

33   The Battle of Limoges happened in August 1370, when the three sons of Edward III, including John of Gaunt, led their English armies in the siege and sacking of the almost undefended town. Hailed as a 'glorious victory' by the English, it saw the slaughter of many hundreds of the civilian population, including children: Froissart's chronicle says 3,000.

such as this (*to* **Elizabeth**). (*Disgusted at himself*) The Devil take my soul, by me as well. (*Weeping, turning to the others who are realising* he *was the rapist and killer. Both now tearful,* **Drummer** *and* **Bartholomew** *grasp hands*) That night, drenched in sin, strong men wept for their imperilled souls, begging Jesus never more will we murder and violate our brothers and sisters; the True Commons. (*Vehemently*) War is the nobles' way, squabbling amongst themselves, spilling our blood for prizes and glory. A wise ruler knows a country thrives not through the sword and knight but the plough and shepherd, brewer and maid, nurturing bounteous nature, bringing forth bread and wool for market. (*Wiping his tears, indicating the tens of thousands surrounding them*) *This* is God's answer to those prayers. (*Agreeing,* **Drummer** *pats* **Bartholomew** *on the shoulder, then, picking up the beat again, marches them back to their places*) The king will hear it. *He* will set things right.

(*All except* **Bartholomew** *sit back as they were.* **Godwin** *and* **Elizabeth** *look to* **Katherine***, who, after consideration, nods* **Bartholomew** *back to his seat*)

Elizabeth

The king?! But he'll never speak to a peasant.

Katherine

(*Drily*) He'll speak to thirty thousand!

(*A tension-releasing laugh*)

Bartholomew

We must have care though. Talk reason and no ill to his honour.

Elizabeth

(*Happy to have something to contribute*) He's young, they say.

Bartholomew

Fourteen. An innocent.

Godwin

(*Chuckling*) I was no innocent at fourteen.

Katherine

(*Laughing too*) Nor I.

Godwin

I would I had met you then. (*Bawdily*) Were you a fine wench?

Katherine

No finer than I am now. And still too good for you!

(*All enjoy this banter except* **Bartholomew**)

Bartholomew

(*Insisting*) King Richard is 'protected', shielded from the strains of leadership by the great lords who should guide him well but abuse the power they have.

Godwin

Like Sudbury. And John O' Gaunt, his uncle.

Katherine

Hobb the Robber too!

Bartholomew

(*Agreeing*) It is *they*, not the king, that hold wages down, raise rents, prevent free movement for those in search of better lives! It is *they*, not King Richard, who make and lose the wars, want more and wrack us for taxes we cannot pay.

(**Fool** *softly does an 'I want a war!' impression of* **King**)

Elizabeth

I heard tell Gaunt has built a great palace.

Katherine

While we rot and starve.

Godwin

(*To* **Bartholomew**) And so? For all these traitors?

Bartholomew

(*Thoughtfully*) For them, yes, a spike, but prudence and no harm to the ...

(*Pats his pockets for a piece of paper. It's handed him by* **Fool**. *Reading*)

'Have enough and say Ho!

And do well and better,[34] and fleeth sin

And seeketh peace, and hold you therein.'[35]

Elizabeth

John Ball's words?

(**Bartholomew** *nods. This is enough to settle the argument for now*)

(*Proudly*) My father is with him. And Wat Tyler. And ... (*shyly*) my Edward. Deciding. They'll do what's best.

Katherine

If they don't, *I'll* tell them.

Godwin

(*Laughs, but with her*) What would you?

Katherine

(*Thinks*) That if *we* have not justice, *they* shall have not peace.

(*This phrase is strangely familiar. In the background,* **Fool** *chants 'No justice—No peace!'* **Katherine** *decides the stew is ready*)

Elizabeth

(*Ladling it out*) How far is London?

Katherine

Less than a day. Came to a market here once, to sell my brew. (*To all around*) There are those that water it, but not I. (*She pours some*) Not fit for one of my fine lords I daresay, but readily made and wholesome.

---

34 'Do well' and 'Do better' are allegorical characters in Piers Plowman.
35 'Hold you therein' is an example of the appeals for restraint, political purpose, and clarity about the aims of the rising.

Bartholomew

(*Strongly, taking the jug from* **Katherine**) No one's to touch a drop. Wat Tyler's orders. Clear heads for a clear purpose.

Godwin

(*Regretfully putting his cup down*) They'd buy it now. To calm their hose-pissing fear.

(*Laughter. They eat. The food is as good as the company.* **Elizabeth**, *to herself at first then accompanied by* **Drummer**, *performs the song* **M2** *was practising as the audience entered. It grows in power, as if the whole of Blackheath is listening. Transfixed, the others fall into a tranquility they have never known. Whatever they may have been or done and had done to them, whatever may be the result of this enterprise, they are here now, united in extraordinary and impossible revolt.* **Godwin** *surreptitiously reaches for his ale but a finger-wagging* **Fool** *has removed it*)

Elizabeth

(*Breaking off suddenly*) Will there be soldiers? At the London gates?

Bartholomew

(*Looking around, smiling*) There are more longbows on this field than Gaunt has fighting Scotland.

Katherine

(*Still annoyed at* **Bartholomew** *for confiscating her brew*) We have right on our side. All we wish is fair treatment.[36]

Bartholomew

Which God and King Richard will give us.

Godwin

And justice served against traitors.

(*Agreement*)

---

36 The ideology of the Revolt was characterised by a tension between the addressing of immediate problems and concrete demands, and a more radical egalitarian ideal that was expressed throughout by the teachings of many of the wandering priests, and particularly John Ball.

Elizabeth

And afterwards ... what?

(**Bartholomew** *thinks hard*)

Katherine

(*Gently mocking to* **Elizabeth, Godwin** *hears too*) He don't know everything then.

Bartholomew

(*Frowns at their laughter, but still has nothing*) Is there more?

(*All consider this*)

Katherine

(*Confidently*) John Ball will know.

(*Agreement. Thoughtful silence. A pause grows too long*)

Fool

(*Sotto voce, growing louder, playing all the roles*)

'It's John Ball!' 'Where?' 'On that mound.' 'I can't see him.' 'There he is.' 'I thought he'd be taller.' 'You're on my foot!' 'Or older.' 'Quiet! He's speaking.'

Godwin

Quick, girl! Up.

(**Elizabeth** *is helped onto* **Godwin's** *shoulders*)

Scene 12

Fool

Placard: '12th of June 1381: John Ball's Speech.'

(*All stare out over the audience's heads*)

Bartholomew

(*To* **Elizabeth**) Can you see him?[37]

---

37 The method of repeated speeches relayed through different sections of the gathering

Katherine

Shh!

Elizabeth

A man. In priest's robes and crook. (**Fool** *takes position stage left, loudly mouthing the 'Fellowship is life ...' line*) He's speaking, but I can't hear ... Ah! Somebody, a woman, is repeating his words. (**Fool** *moves centre stage, becoming this woman, speaking the line more audibly*) Oh I see ... (*To* **Campfire Comrades** *only*) 'Fellowship is life and lack of fellowship is death.'[38]

(*Exasperated,* **Fool** *becomes another crowd member stage right or in the audience, calling 'Speak up!'*)

(*Broadcasting to the next campfires*) 'Fellowship is life and lack of fellowship is death. (**Fool** *must go rapidly back and forth, beginning and repeating on the next lines until* **Elizabeth** *is delivering the speech fluently and powerfully*) In Hell, there is no answer to man's cry for help because there is no brotherhood, but every man for himself. If God would have had any bondmen from the beginning, *He* would have appointed who should be bond and who free. When Adam delved and Eve span—who was then the gentleman? (**Fool** *encourages audience participation, repeating if necessary*) Matters cannot go well in England, nor ever shall until all things be held in common, when there are no vassals or lords.'

(*Rising to a crescendo*)

'And therefore, I exalt you to consider that now the time is come, appointed to us by God in which ye may, if ye will, cast off the yoke of bondage and recover liberty!'

(*As* **Elizabeth**, *triumphant*) Brothers! Sisters! Tomorrow. (*All raise their fists*) London and Good King Richard!

(*All exit cheering, led by* **Drummer. Fool** *remains, a satisfied expression turning thoughtful*)

---

has been used in many such historical episodes.
38   These words quoting John Ball's speech can be found today on a plaque at the Church of The Ascension at Blackheath.

Scene 13

Fool

Placard: '13th of June, Rotherhithe: King Richard on a Boat Meeting Wat Tyler's Peasant Army.'

(*The nobles on board ship in painful silence. At last,* **M3** *has bishop's mitre placed on their head by* **Fool**: *'It's Sudbury time!'* **Sudbury** *appears; oily and corrupt, fervently praying.* **Walworth** *obsessively sharpens his dagger.* **Salisbury** *is running possibilities in his head, weighing up actions and consequences, whether* **King** *is up to the job.* **King** *is childishly furious at being there at all*)

King

(*To* **Salisbury**) You are looking at me. Say something.

Salisbury

(*To* **King**) Have you practised the words we discussed?

Walworth

A king should not waste breath on these scoundrels!

Sudbury

Or pay ear to what they ask. What right have these ... farmyard beasts to speak to us?

Salisbury

(*Drily*) The right of thirty thousand.

King

So many?

(*Behind them,* **Fool** *quickly raises the 'Probably' placard. All turn but it is gone*)

Salisbury

Are you prepared, your Majesty? Or should I ..?

King

I am king. I can do anything. But remind me *why* I am doing *this*.

Salisbury

Again? (*Controlling his exasperation*) We are ... seeking time, your Majesty, observing their weakness and strength. (*With a pointed look at* **Walworth**) They *have* leaders, or such a rabble could not have done so much so quickly. Ball we know. We must identify these others. Cut off the head, and the serpent withers quickly. Therefore we will discover their wishes, if necessary pay heed to some few of their demands ...

Sudbury

(*Quickly*) But not grant them.

Salisbury

It may be ... *prudent* to make such promises as ...

Sudbury

(*Quickly*) But not keep them.

Walworth

Shall we serve them dinner too? Wipe their shit-caked arses after? (*Practises the killing thrust*) Majesty, here are four ships with knights close to. Let me land with them and hack these rebels to offal.

King

Silence, Walworth and for God's sake put away that weapon!

(**Walworth** *reluctantly sheathes the dagger*)

(*To* **Salisbury**) And *then* everything will be as it was? I can have my war?

Salisbury

(*Exchanging a look with* **Walworth**. *It is so past that moment*) Exactly, your Majesty.

Fool

A jest, masters, to lighten the mood. (*Characters exit when mentioned*) A king, his advisors and a petrified Archbishop of Canterbury are being rowed in a rickety boat towards thousands of furious, well-armed peasants when the king says ... he says ... (*to audience*) you'll like this one ... he says ... I'm sorry, I've got nothing. Oh, look! (**Fool** *steps aside to reveal, amongst 30,000 peasants massed at the shore, the* **Campfire Comrades**) Peasants. Revolting! See what I did there?

Scene 14

(*The* **Campfire Comrades**, *vying to see and hear*)

Elizabeth

Is that the king's boat? (**Fool** '*corrects*' **M5** *looking in the wrong direction*) Has he really come? Will he speak to us?

Katherine

With Wat Tyler. See him making his way to the bankside.

(*They crane their necks the other way.* **Fool** '*corrects*' **M5** *again*)

Bartholomew

Petty lords or advisors. They would never send the king himself into such danger.

Katherine

Kill them then, who advise him so ill and show his honest people such scorn.

Godwin

Who will they send? Sudbury?

Elizabeth

(*Fearful/angry*) Hobb the Robber?

Godwin

Kill him. Kill Sudbury! Sudbury! (*shouts excitedly*) Give us Sudbury!

(*A roar goes up, 'Give us Sudbury! Kill Sudbury!, etc'*)

Scene 15

(**Campfire Comrades** *continue chanting until each freezes into noble character position, aghast at the army of peasants waiting for them.* **Katherine** *lets out a blood curdling 'Kiiill Suuudbury!' during which* **Fool** *plants* **Sudbury's** *mitre on her*)

Sudbury

May God preserve us!

Walworth

You had better hope so.

King

(*Gagging*) That stench! Is it ..?

(**Fool** *mimes* **Sudbury** *has soiled himself. The smell is not* **Sudbury** *but the peasants, drawing ever closer*[39])

Sudbury

(*On his knees before* **King**) Save me, Richard! Have I not been your most loyal and obedient servant. Do not cast me to these savages. I beg of you. Your Majesty, *swear* that you will not ...

Walworth

(*To* **Sudbury**) Compose yourself, cur! Nobility must *not* be seen so.

King

(*Shocked*) They are armed! Why? Do they not love me?

(*Behind them* **Fool** *is making silent 'Yes, it's Sudbury' shouts to peasants, pointing and mouthing 'Here he is.'*)

Fool

Maybe it's just a lower-class way of showing it, Sire? (*Declaiming*) Oh, Archbishop of Canterbury, Sudbury; with your lavish and

---

39 June, July and August of 1381, the records tell us, was a freak summer, with long and blisteringly hot days.

ornate church decorations, vast, enormously expensive to build and maintain cathedrals, huge landholdings, fine, gold-threaded silk vestments and exquisite diamond- and ruby-encrusted ecclesiastical jewellery. (*Rapidly, like a financial ad disclaimer*) That our backbreaking and thankless toil has paid for and is fully justified in the Bible somewhere, which we could read for ourselves if it was written in a language we could understand and anyway weren't illiterate peasant scum. (*After taking a well-earned breath and bow to the audience,* **Fool** *mimes decapitating* **Sudbury***, picking up the severed head and kissing it on the lips*) How we adore you!

(**King** *laughs,* **Walworth** *is bitterly amused.* **Salisbury** *is not*)

Sudbury

(*Terrified*) Tell the oarsmen to stop! Turn the boat around.

Salisbury

(*Controlling his emotions*) Your Majesty must stand firm now. Address your people.

(**King** *shakily steps onto the prow of the ship*)

King

If this does not work, Salisbury, I shall sharpen your executioner's axe myself.

(**King** *summons the courage to speak. Just as he is about to begin,* **Drummer** *signals scene change. Frustration from* **M2** *'But I was about to …'*)

Scene 16

(*The* **Campfire Comrades***, craning to see and hear*)

Bartholomew

It *is* the king.

Katherine

How do you know?

Bartholomew

See the White Hart pennant.[40] King Richard's arms. The cowards!

Godwin

Good. The boy king will listen and make things right.

Elizabeth

(**M2** *late getting into position*) Have we won then? Will there be justice?

Godwin

To think I have lived to see this day.

Katherine

(*Reacting to* **Elizabeth** *and* **Godwin**) We've done nothing yet.

Elizabeth

Those other boats. Why do they glint so?

Bartholomew

Knights! Why has the king brought weapons with him? We mean *him* no harm.

Godwin

Suuudbury!

Bartholomew

He's about to speak. Look at him. Incredible! Richard! Our *King* Richard!

Elizabeth

Those fine clothes, the crown. Oh, how beautiful! (**Elizabeth** *weeps and has to be held up.* **Bartholomew** *falls to his knees*)

Godwin

(*Aghast*) What are you doing?

---

40   The White Hart (the white stag) was an ancient symbol from Arthurian legend, adopted as a personal badge by Richard II.

Katherine

Get off your knees.

Bartholomew

The king! (**Elizabeth** *joins his roar of praise. 'The king! Richard! The king!'*)

Katherine

(*Pointing over the heads of the audience. This time* **M5** *knows which direction*) Over there. Tyler. Tyler! (*like 'Oh Jeremy Corbyn'*) Oh-oh Wat Tyler!

(*All join in. Fool encourages audience participation*)

Scene 17

(**Elizabeth, Godwin** and **Bartholomew** *chant until each switches role to become noble;* **King** *on the prow steeling himself to speak.* **Katherine**, *letting out a particularly loud—'Oh-oh Wat … is 'dressed' by* **Fool** *as* **Wat Tyler** *on the river bank.* **Fool** *goes to* **Wat Tyler's** *side, 'becoming' 30,000 peasants*)

King

(*Barely getting the words out*) Sirs, tell me what you want.

Fool

(*To audience, indicating* **King**) His actual words! (*'Probably' placard*)

Wat Tyler

(*Confident and jovial, aware of his huge audience*) We wish thee to land where we will remonstrate and tell thee more at our ease what our wants are.

Fool

(*Indicating* **Wat Tyler**) And his!

(*As Peasants. 'Nice one, Wat'. 'We want Sudbury, etc.'*)

King

(*Smiling emptily, turning back to the nobles.* **Salisbury** *has not prepared him for this*) What do I say?

Fool

(*Watching keenly. Aside to audience*) We're making it up now!

Salisbury

(*At a loss/realising this wasn't such a good idea after all*) I ... don't ...

King

(*To* **Wat Tyler**) It ...would be more seemly were you to come to me.

Salisbury

(*Exchanging a panicked look with* **Walworth**) What? No!

Wat Tyler

As you wish, Sire. (*joking, performing to* **Fool/Peasants** *who love this*) Pull your ship closer that I and some few of my merry fellows may step aboard.

King

I ... very well. (*To the alarm of the other nobles*) Oarsmen, draw nearer the shore.

Fool

(*As 30,000 peasants, with laughter and enthusiasm*) 'What's happening?' 'Don't do it Wat!' 'Is that Sudbury?' 'Get him?' 'We're coming with you.' 'On board!' 'Do I have too? I get sea sick.' 'Everyone aboard!'

King

(*To nobles*) Do they laugh at me!? (*To* **Wat Tyler**/*audience*) How dare you laugh in the presence of your ...

Walworth

The dogs! (*Hissing to* **Salisbury**) Get Richard out of there, now!

Salisbury

(**Walworth** *drags* **King** *down.* **Salisbury** *gets up with difficulty*)

Gentlemen, you are ... (*desperately thinking*) not properly dressed, nor in a fit condition to talk with the king.[41]

Fool

(*To audience*) 'Not properly dressed!' Honestly, that's what Salisbury said! (*gets the audience to join in 'Probably'*)

Salisbury

(*To oarsmen*) Make speed. Away! Away![42]

Scene 18

(**Campfire Comrades**, *mocking each other's clothing, etc.*)

Godwin

Wait. What's happening?

Elizabeth

Is Wat Tyler boarding? John Ball? Can anybody see? Is my father with them? Edward?

Katherine

The boats ... are turning.

Bartholomew

The king is leaving?! They are taking him away.

Katherine

(*Calling after the boats*) Cowards! Traitors!

(*All watch the boats recede*)

---

41 These absurd words to the rebels by Salisbury are reported in the chronicle by Froissart.
42 The chronicle by Froissart reports that the royal group, stunned by the encounter, were rowed back to the Tower of London with not a word spoken between them.

Elizabeth

He wouldn't speak with us? How can he listen to our demands?

Bartholomew

He would. Those others stole him back.

Godwin

That *was* Sudbury! I could smell his fear of justice.

Elizabeth

All this way for that?

Katherine

If they won't bring the traitors to us, we'll have to win them ourselves.

Bartholomew

Aye. Onwards. To London!

All

To London!

Scene 19

Fool

Placard: 'King Richard in the Tower of London.'

(*A tiny, cramped room at the highest point of the completely surrounded Tower, windows on all sides from which the nobles stare fearfully out. All except* **Fool** *arrive breathless from a long and rapid climb*)

King

When I said I wanted a war, I meant with France, not my own stinking peasants. Where's the honour in that?

Fool

(*To audience*) Or any hope of winning?

King

(*Furious*) They laughed. At me!

Salisbury

(*Gasping for breath*) Your ... Majesty, we must take care in considering our next ...

King

Nobody laughs *at* the king.

Walworth

Damn ... right!

Sudbury

(*Arriving last, dishevelled and terrified, closing the door but finding no key to lock it*) They stormed the London gates!

Salisbury

No need. (*Wryly*) They were never locked.

Walworth

(*Pointing out of a window in horror*) Burning my houses!

King

(*Jumping up and down*) I want to burn them all! Laughing at me. Telling *me* what to do! No one tells me what to do.

Walworth

(*Shouting from the window*) No one tells the King what to do. (*To* **King**) Sit down your Majesty.

King

(*Sits but there is no* **M3** *and falls. There are no servants to pick* **King** *up. Eventually,* **Fool** *does it*) At what point did they not understand that I am the king.

Walworth

A hundred men is all we need. Turn the Thames into a river of blood.

Salisbury

Ours if you listen to him, your ...

King

I want to crush them.

Walworth

My houses!

Salisbury

(*Aside to* **Walworth**) Not everything is about your brothels, Walworth.

Sudbury

Indeed, there are far more important things.

Walworth

(*To* **Sudbury**) My Lord Archbishop has not *always* thought so.

Salisbury

(*Putting himself before* **King**) All our efforts now must be to preserve your safety. To keep you on the throne.

King

Which, so far, have led to me being ridiculed by a hoard of verminous peasants! (*Running to several windows; others must get out of his way*) Where are *my* armies? Don't I have any?

Walworth

(*Proudly*) Three, Sire. The finest bodies of men to be found in Christendom.

King

(*Pointedly, looking out of a window*) The Tower is surrounded by peasants.

Fool

(*Interrupting happily*) Oh, not just peasants, Sire.

King

What?

Fool

(*Pointing out of different windows*) Artisans, tradespeople, small merchants,[43] not to mention a considerable number of Londoners, who hate you lot (*tailing off*) just ... as ... much. (*Drumming stops. To audience, didactically*) Strictly speaking, 'peasants'' revolt is something of a misnomer. Really it should be 'The 1381 Uprising of the Lower Orders' or 'Rebellion of a Variety of Oppressed Social Classes'. Not as zingy though, is it? (**Ms** *glare at* **Fool**) Sorry, just ... there could be educated people in the house ... (**Ms** *appraise the audience doubtfully. Drumming resumes. To* **Salisbury** *and* **Walworth**, *fake-offended on behalf of* **King**) Gentlemen, my royal master has demanded of you where are his armies?

Salisbury

(*Reluctantly, looking daggers at* **Fool**) One is with John of Gaunt, in the north. I'm sure as soon as he is informed, he will ... (*not sounding so sure*) *immediately* march.[44] (*To* **King**) That is why, at all costs, we must delay...

King

The others?

Salisbury

(*Unhappily*) Buckingham's men (*preventing* **Fool** *from repeating their mummery of Buckingham's disastrous defeat and surrender*) are still 'resting' in Wales.

King

And the third?

Walworth

Yes, where *is* the gallant Earl of Cambridge?

---

43 'Peasants' should be understood in a general sense of the 'common people' rather than an exact description of social class. In fact, there were many tradespeople, petty merchants, and craft workers that made up the march to London, along with the land workers of Essex and Kent.

44 Whilst John of Gaunt's army was a long way off in Scotland, it was also the case that his loyalty to the king was not assured. Gaunt had his own ambitions to the throne of England.

Salisbury

(*Frantically signalling to* **Walworth** *to drop it*) His Majesty has no time to hear ...

King

Somebody had better tell me where the Earl of Cambridge and his army are when they should be here protecting me.

(**Fool** *steps forward.* **Salisbury** *would silence them but* **King** *wants to hear*)

Fool

(*To audience, laughs*) True story. (*To* **King**) My noble earl *was* in Plymouth, Sire. Inclement seas prevented his sailing for adventure and conquest in Portugal.

King

(*Triumphantly to* **Salisbury**) And you would have me converse with pigs in the sty. Cambridge is no doubt slaughtering the rabble at my gates as we speak.

(**King** *looks hopefully from several windows, disgusted by the sight and smell, then back at* **Salisbury**, *who continues to look embarrassed*)

Salisbury

(*Threateningly, as* **Fool** *opens their mouth*) Do not ..!

King

Silence, you old fool! (*To* **Fool**) Tell me.

Fool

(*Shrugging*) The noble earl judged the tempest at sea more inviting than that at home.

King

(*Not getting it*) And ..?

Fool

On receiving the royal summons, he and his entire army set sail immediately. (**Sudbury** *starts to weep.* **King** *still doesn't understand*)

For *Portugal*, not ... (*Speaking to a toddler*) He isn't coming.

King

(*Desperately*) Reserves? Retired soldiers? My father had them keep their weapons.

Fool

(*Looking out*) Longbows, swords, axes. Freshly sharpened I'd say. (**King** *is initially pleased, then realises*)

Sudbury

(*At another window*) The servants are saying they mean to destroy the Savoy.

Walworth

A hundred and fifty. Brave men and true.

Sudbury

(*To* **King**) If you cannot protect your uncle's great palace, they could kill us all.

Salisbury

(*Cutting across the tumult*) Which is why we must give them what they want.

(*Stunned silence. This is heresy*)

Fool

(*Sotto voce, as the crowd*) We want Sudbury! We want Sudbury!

(*Behind* **Sudbury**, **Walworth** *draws his dagger, looking to* **Salisbury** *who shakes his head 'not yet'.* **Walworth** *reluctantly sheathes the blade*)

King

(*Not meeting* **Sudbury's** *eye*) That is ... absolutely *not* going to happen.

Sudbury

(*On his knees, grasping for the* **King's** *hands*) It mustn't!

Salisbury

But it *is* what you are going to *say*.

King

I will *not* meet with them again. (*Looking disgustedly at* **Sudbury**, *cringing at his feet*) It's not... *natural*.

Salisbury

Sire. Tomorrow, you will find the king inside you. Full of benevolence, who listens to his good and loyal subjects seeking justice which (*glancing at* **Sudbury**) only you can give them.

Walworth

(*Laughs bitterly*) Richard the second. The Plantagenet who gave his throne to a peasant! Is that how you wish tomorrow to record you?

Salisbury

If we don't promise them what they want today, there will be no tomorrow.

Walworth

(*Weakly*) Two hundred men.

King

(*Looking out of a window, finally seeing what is there. To* **Walworth**) We haven't fifty. (*Moving to* **Salisbury**) What do we do?

Salisbury

At this moment, three hundred men or Gaunt's or Cambridges' entire army would be swept aside. There are *thirty thousand* out there. It matters not if Walworth or Salisbury or Sudbury (**Sudbury** *is not so sure*) endure but Richard will. King*ship* shall.

Sudbury

(*To* **Walworth** *while* **King** *is hearing* **Salisbury's** *plan*) I had him in my Maidstone gaol. Ball. Before that rebel scum took it. My God! If I only had him now. (**Fool** *plays a commiserating violin*) I would tear out his entrails, scatter his butchered carcass to the four corners of the …

Walworth

That impudent rascal Wat Tyler too. Why he spoke to his Majesty as if they pissed in the same … (*interrupting* **Salisbury**) And *you* would have us …

Salisbury

(*To* **King**, *ignoring* **Walworth**) These are simple folk who love and trust you. They will have their 'day', Sire. Serve 'justice' upon a few traitors (*another glance at* **Sudbury**), we can scarce deny it. Afterwards, your promises in their pockets, they must disperse *separately* to their fields. Then Ball, Wat Tyler, every man, woman and child. Cut into a thousand pieces.

(*Convinced,* **King** *exits through a different door, with* **Walworth** *close behind*)

(*Sharply ordering* **Fool** *before they can follow*) Have Hobb the … Sir Robert Hales brought up here.

Fool

(*Bowing elaborately*) At once, your Noble-ship.(**Salisbury** *moves to follow* **King**. **Fool** *coughs*) Thirty thousand peasants? (**Fool** *plays a peasant crashing in the door, axe raised, 'Kiiill Sudbury!'* **Salisbury** *watches but doesn't react.* **Fool** *holds out a hand for a key*) Shouldn't we lock the door?

Salisbury

(*With a sneer at the fervently praying* **Sudbury** *and a calculating smile at the audience,* **Salisbury** *pats the key still in his pocket*) That won't be necessary.

(**Fool** *bows again.* **Salisbury** *leaves the same way as* **King**)

Fool

(*Lifting the mitre from* **Sudbury's** *head*) You won't be needing that anymore.[45]

---

45 Simon Sudbury, the Archbishop of Canterbury, was captured by the rebels with

(**M3** *grins at the audience, slicing a finger across their throat*)

(*To audience*) Meanwhile. A mile and a half upstream. No justice? No peace.

Scene 20

Fool

Placard: 'The Sacking of John O' Gaunt's Great New Palace, The Savoy'[46]

Wat Tyler

'None, on pain to lose his head, should presume to convert to their own use anything that there is or might be found, but that they should break such plate and vessels of gold and silver, as were in that house in great plenty, into small pieces. Clothes of gold and silver and silk and velvet, they should tear; rings and jewels set with precious stones they should break into mortars, that they might be of no use, and throw the same into the Thames or into privies.'

(*Holding the clearly labelled 'eyewitness account'*, **Fool** *looks round but there is no available* **Mechanical**. **Drummer** *points to their drum, 'I don't do acting.'* **Fool** *threatens to 'make' them.* **Drummer** *reluctantly reads, by the end thoroughly enjoying it*)

Drummer

(*Reading the* **'Eyewitness'** *account*)

'They took all the torches they could find, and lighted them, and burnt all the sheets and coverlets and beds and headboards of great worth. All the napery and other things that they could

---

Robert Hales at the Tower of London, and beheaded. His mitre was nailed to his head to keep it from falling after it was displayed on the walls of the Tower of London

46 The burning down of the Savoy, John of Gaunt's palace, was a hugely symbolic moment in the rising, a calculated insult to Gaunt's power and wealth, and to the rich more generally. Froissart tells us that the palace was destroyed systematically, stick-by-stick, treasure-by-treasure, so that nothing was left. Looting was not allowed.

discover, they carried to the hall and set on fire with their torches. They burnt the hall, and the chambers, and all the buildings within the gates. They found three barrels of gunpowder, and thinking it gold or silver, cast it into the fire. The powder exploded, setting the hall in a greater blaze than before, to the great loss and damage of the Duke of Lancaster.'[47]

Bartholomew

The Savoy palace! Jesus, did you see that stuff? Glass![48] It's hard. You can see through it! When it smashes, the pieces cut like razors. Plates. Yellow. Gold! They eat off gold! It felt good when we burned things. But it was too much.

Katherine

God could not allow such injustice. Poor folk starving whilst such a palace exists! Says good John Ball, this is *not* God's work. Therefore, it be the work of the Devil, and would it not be God's work to tear it down? Aye, says I.

Godwin

Gold, jewels, softest pillows you ever saw. Set light to me ballocks, and I could still sleep on those. Touch a thing, they said, and it's your head. They meant it too; one lad got the chop.[49] Sliced up the gold and threw it in the Thames! Criminal it was. I'm coming back one day with a fishing rod. Couple of trout might have swallowed something.

Elizabeth

At home we use fire for life. To cook with, to light and heat in winter. It is a power of life given us by God. It made our home. When I first saw the Savoy; a palace, not a home, as empty and useless as a cold hearth. We used fire that day. I remember

---

47 This passage comes from the *Anonomalle Chronicle*.
48 Fine glass objects were valuable luxury items. They would likely have been imported from Venice, the centre of glassmaking at this time.
49 Wat Tyler was a stern commander who allowed no such behaviour that might have distracted from the aims of the rising. The chronicle by Froissart tells us that one man was executed for looting.

the smoke catch the back of my throat, scrubbing my insides, scouring out the devil. The most beautiful thing I ever saw was this beautiful thing burning.

(*All turn to look, intrigued, at* **Elizabeth**, *who with more confidence repeats her last line.* **Katherine** *tries it out, feeling how it sounds, before happily agreeing. Then* **Godwin**. **Bartholomew** *struggles but finally assents. The line becomes a round/monk's incantation/barbershop chorus, whichever is most joyful*)

All

The most beautiful thing we ever saw was this beautiful thing burning!

Scene 21

Fool

Placard: '14th of June, Mile End: King Richard Signing Manumissions for Every Town and Village in England.'[50]

(*Whilst parading, to a puzzled audience member*) Manumission? Means ... ah, read your programme!

(**King** *with* **Salisbury** *and* **Fool**. **Wat Tyler** *enters with* **Peasant 1** *who conceals two placards.* **Tyler** *spits on a palm and holds it out to* **King**. **Peasant 1** *shares amazement and admiration with audience.* **King** *refuses the hand.* **Fool** *points out the* '**Wat Tyler's Kent army of 30,000**' *placard now being held up by* **Peasant 1**. **King** *still not keen. Placard* '**Jack Straw's Essex army of 30,000**' *is revealed. Both turned to read* '**Grrrr!**', *jiggled up and down.* **King** *is ready to deal.* **Wat Tyler** *offers* **King** *the peasants' demands. He won't touch them.* **Salisbury** *takes them, reads one, barely controlling himself and passes them to* **Fool**. **Tyler** *jovially pats* **King** *hard on the back. As* **Fool** *reads,* **Peasant 1** *becomes a succession of caricatured peasants with their village's manumission document.* **Fool** *encourages the audience to cheer every time one is signed and each peasant raises it high.* **King** *controls*

---

50   The *Anonomalle Chronicle* describes rows of tables, each staffed all of that day by a legal scribe, with village delegations queuing at each station for their manumissions or Charters of Freedom.

his disgust as **Salisbury** *reassures*)

Fool

(*To audience*) Actual peasant demands.[51] Prob ... no, really! 'Each man shall be beholden only to himself and no man shall be bonded to his lord.'

(**King** *signs a document*)

'No one of the rebels shall be punished for their actions in the rising for they acted in the name of justice and right was on their side.'

(**King** *signs*)

'All peasants be granted the right to sell their produce in the fairs and markets and whichever town and borough they choose.'

(**King** *signs*)

'Land rent shall be set at fourpence an acre.'

(*The last peasant carries* **Sudbury's** *head, 'accidentally' presenting it instead of their document.* **Fool** *to audience 'not really!' The 'mistake' is corrected.* **King** *signs and the peasant leaves, kissing the head like a sports trophy and leading a triumphant 'When Adam delved' ... chant with the audience.* **King** *glares, speechlessly furious, at* **Salisbury**)

Salisbury

Tomorrow, your Majesty.

Scene 22

(**Campfire Comrades** *full of the energy they had after burning the Savoy, ready to resume the Revolt; this reflected by Drumming. They begin a 'When Adam delved ...' chant but* **Fool** *intervenes, instructing* **Drummer** *in a sombre tone*)

Fool

---

51 These were the rebel demands presented to Richard II at Mile End. They amounted to a general demand for an end to feudalism and the economic regulation of land-work.

Placard: 'One Week After the Defeat of the Peasants' Revolt.'

(**Ms** *confused. 'But a minute ago we were storming the ...'* **Fool** *points to where they've got to in the script.* **Ms** *shrug, disappointed.* **Fool** *reads placard again with emphasis on 'Defeat'.* **Drummer** *recommences. A different, colder camp. Slowly and painfully,* **Elizabeth** *and* **Katherine**, *then* **Godwin**, *carrying* **Sudbury's** *head which he dumps beside him, and lastly* **Bartholomew**, *enter fearfully from different directions.* **Katherine** *glares angrily at* **Bartholomew**)

Bartholomew

(*Unfurling his tattered manumission document*) Freedom! The king's promise. In writing. He would have kept it, but we pushed too far, asked for too much.

Godwin

Wat Tyler wasn't a man to stop asking.

Elizabeth

Should he have?

Katherine

(*Angry/bitter*) If the cowards and (*to* **Bartholomew**) simpletons hadn't gone home so fast, we could have made the boy king keep his word.[52]

Bartholomew

(*Unable to understand it himself*) We'd won! Burned their palaces, executed the traitors. Wasn't that what we came for? Crops aren't going to harvest themselves. Tyler and Ball. They never should have ...

Katherine

(*One of the most important lines of the play*) The moment you stop shouting for more is the moment they take everything back.

---

52 Once the rebels began to return to their homes and fields, King Richard's repression began.

Godwin

They took Tyler. Right before our eyes.

Bartholomew

We demanded too much!

Katherine

We demanded too little!

Godwin

We *demanded*!

Elizabeth

(*Looks at them, disbelieving, slight smile*)

And they listened!

Scene 23

Fool

Placard: '15th of June, Westminster: King Richard Praying Before his Betrayal and Murder of Wat Tyler.'[53]

(**King** *on his knees, praying.* **Walworth** *and* **Salisbury** *enter.* **Drummer** *pulls* **Fool** *back from joining them. They watch from 'outside' the scene*)

Salisbury

(*Poorly controlling his glee*) They have agreed, your Majesty. Tyler wishes to present more demands.

Walworth

Filth! (*Realises this is a church. Under his breath*) Scum!

King

(*Disbelieving*) More?! What more is there?

---

53 Richard II would later claim divine blessing for his reign because he had prayed at Westminster before the murder of Tyler. This is expressed in the symbolism of the Wilton Diptych that can be seen at the British National Portrait Museum.

Salisbury

This is *precisely* what I ... *we* schemed for, your Majesty. Gulled with your promises, the Essex peasants have departed. Only Tyler and his Kentish rebels remain.[54]

(**King** *resumes praying*)

Walworth

We must dress you in your armour, Sire. A cloak to cover it.[55] I have assembled a loyal force.[56] (**King** *does not move*) The thing is planned but ... dangerous.

King

How large a force?

(**Walworth** *exchanges a glance with* **Salisbury**)

Salisbury

Play your part, Sire. 'Good' King Richard, innocent of blood. As long as the common herd continue to trust that, the day will yet be ours.

King

Leave me. (*They are reluctant*) I will come. (*As they are almost gone*) Where?

Salisbury

(*Almost laughing*) Smithfield.[57]

(**King** *prays a few moments longer*)

---

54 The Essex rebels were the first to return to their villages with their Charters of Freedom. The Kent rebels, less tied to the manorial system and to the village fields, were more politically aware, less trusting of the promises they had been given and more radical in their demands.

55 Froissart describes how the royal group prepared for the meeting at Smithfield, putting on armour beneath their outer robes, planning their assassination of the rebel leaders.

56 In the time they had bought, Sir Robert Knowles had assembled a force of eight thousand that would be loyal to the King.

57 Smithfield was a slaughtering field for cattle and sheep, giving the location a grim irony, not lost on the nobles.

Scene 24

(*The 'one week after' camp*)

Godwin

I said, d'you remember? Isn't that the place they slaughter beasts?

Katherine

We should have known.

Elizabeth

He went alone? Wat Tyler.

Godwin

A mire of blood and mud.

Bartholomew

A thousand bows went with him. But he bade us wait apart. So as not to frighten the king.

Katherine

We stopped shouting.

Godwin

Just a boy. It should have been so easy. How could we fail?

Scene 25

Fool

Placard: '15th of June: King Richard's Betrayal and Murder of Wat Tyler.'

(*Drumming resumes the celebratory tempo of* Scene 21. **Fool** *jumps up, part of the action again.* **King** *and* **Salisbury** *stand waiting.* **Wat Tyler** *enters, bidding* **Bartholomew** *to stand apart with bow raised.* **Bartholomew** *holds the pose then becomes* **Walworth**. **Wat Tyler**, *swaggering, hands another document to* **Fool**)

Fool

(*To audience*) The peasants' actual demands![58] (*Theatrically, using the licence the* **Fool** *role gives to mock and challenge the nobles with* **John Ball/Wat Tyler's** *feudal-shattering, revolutionary ideas*) 'Let no law but the Law of Winchester[59] prevail, and let no man be made an outlaw by the decree of judges and lawyers. No lord shall exercise lordship over the Commons.'

Salisbury

(*To* **King**, *with a grim chuckle*) An end to kingship!

Fool

'And since we are oppressed by so vast a hoard of bishops and clerks, let there be but one bishop in England.'

Salisbury

(*To* **King**) The 'hedgerow' priest, John Ball!

Fool

'The property and the goods of the holy Church should be taken and divided according to the needs of the people in each parish, after making provision for the existing clergy and monks, and finally let there be no more villeins in England, but all to be free and of one condition.'[60]

Wat Tyler

A toast, my good lords. King Richard and the True Commons!

(**Fool** *fills glasses.* **Wat Tyler**, *oblivious, quaffs, strutting around the space.* **King** *and* **Salisbury** *sip warily, exchanging glances*)

---

58   The demands at Smithfield went much further than those put the previous day at Mile End. They contain the much more radical thinking of the Kentish rebels and reflect some of the levelling sentiments of John Ball and his followers.

59   The 1285 Law of Winchester of Edward I had enshrined local courts and law enforcement under the system of the Watch and Ward and allowed the population to be armed.

60   The demand for all the wealth of the church to be taken away and redistributed was especially radical and reflected the opposition to the church at this time as a hugely powerful and wealthy institution, able to raise its own taxes and supporting the power of Rome in England.

Walworth

(*A bad actor*) I will not touch this *outlaw's* brew.

Wat Tyler

What's that?

Salisbury

(*A better one, spitting*) Poison! He means to kill the King!

Wat Tyler

Gentlemen! This is as honest an ale as England can serve.

Walworth

Liar! Villain! Murderous, thieving rascal!

Wat Tyler

(*To* **King**) Majesty, calm your dogs. (**Salisbury** *stays* **Walworth's** *hand at this insult*) I have a thousand men in bowshot.

King

(**King** *raises his cup.* **Walworth** *and* **Salisbury** *watch. Will* **King** *play his part?*)

(*Drinks. Spits*) He means to kill me!

(*This next action very fast. Seeing how it is,* **Wat Tyler** *draws his dagger. It is what* **Salisbury** *has been waiting for.* **Walworth** *gets the nod*)

Walworth

A blade! In the presence of the king. Assassin![61]

(**Walworth** *strikes his long-practiced blow. Stabbed from all sides,* **Wat Tyler** *falls*)

Bartholomew

(*To audience, bow raised, peering ahead*) It was too far away.[62] Was it Tyler who had fallen or ..? Then, galloping towards us ... the king!

---

61 The drawing of a blade in the presence of the king was a cause for immediate execution.
62 On that very hot and bright June day, the sun would have been blinding, glinting off

(**King** *strides forward, brushing aside the toy horse* **Fool** *offers*)

King

(*Addressing the audience as peasants*)

(*Haltingly at first, aware there is no* **Salisbury** *or* **Walworth** *at his side, then growing stronger*) There has been a misunderstanding, a terrible mistake. Your leader, Wat Tyler has been ... hurt. I have ... ordered him taken to a hospital. Lower your bows, I beg of you. Be led by me, your good King Richard.

Bartholomew

(*Draws back his bowstring, but confused*)

(*To audience, anguished*) We could trust our king ... couldn't we? It was brave, riding towards us. Alone. A child, almost. And I'd sworn never again would I ...

King

(*With a growing confidence, becoming a* **King**) You have come in righteous anger, and I have listened. Come with me now. Lower your bows. In peace, be led. Away from here, to a place we may speak together.

Bartholomew

How *could* we shoot? To what end? Wat Tyler, our leader, was ...

King

Your king thanks you. (*Kindly*) Trust in him. Come now. In peace. Away.

(**King** *leads off. Bow lowered;* **Bartholomew** *remains*)

Scene 26

(*The 'one week after' camp*)[63]

---

swords, shields, and armour.
63   The final battles of the Revolt took place at North Walsham on 26 June and at Billericay, where 500 rebels were massacred on 28 June 1381.

Godwin

Once, working at my plough, I made the lord's son roar. Pulled one of my faces when he and his pals trotted by on their ponies. (*Pulls the face*) Even the father smiled. Warmed me better than mutton stew. Three weeks ago, I was sticking the same man's guts on my pike. (*Shakes head in confusion*) Now I tremble again at every horseshoe and bridle clink.

Katherine

(*Bitterly to* **Bartholomew**, *still in pose*) You should have loosed your fucking bows!

Bartholomew

(*Shaken from his reverie*) Killed the king, the mayor of London, near every personage in the country! Likely innocents besides. Then what?

Katherine

That many fewer leeches.

Godwin

They'd have made another King.

Katherine

Keep on 'til there are none left. 'When Adam delved and ...'

Bartholomew

(*Angrily, throwing his bow down*) I told you I've seen enough of it! It's one thing to destroy. Who's to build the world anew?

Elizabeth

(*Thoughtfully*) Us. The same that built the last. Laid the stones, mined the iron, embroidered the silk, sowed and harvested the grain, tended the bull, and had it all taken away. From our children too. They have every need of us. What have we for kings?

Godwin

Aye! An axe for every one of them.

Bartholomew

Tell that to Wat Tyler, whose head furnishes the tower gates. Tell that to this girl's father.

(**Katherine** *angrily hushes him and he regrets what he has said, but* **Elizabeth** *continues to look thoughtful*)

Elizabeth

(*Stands unsteadily. Refusing support*)

At the Savoy. Edward ... We come from different villages and our lords would never have allowed us to ... I said, 'follow me.' Took him to one of the bedrooms. He whispered, 'I've never ...' 'Nor I,' I said. We lay on silk. Silk! Cloth, like water through your fingers. You cannot imagine how soft ... Afterwards others came and tore to pieces all the finery and we gladly joined them. Though Edward may be dead and my father too. I lay on silk. (*closes her hands over her belly, strongly*) And one day my child may too.

Godwin

(*Grinning*) It was a good day out all right! And (*Chucking* **Sudbury's** *chin*) no dream for once!

(*Dropping the head,* **Godwin** *fondly takes his leave.* **Elizabeth** *exits too, beckoning* **Katherine** *who first embraces a distraught* **Bartholomew** *who then also leaves*)

Katherine

(*To audience*) We'd been sleeping all our lives, and this was waking up or maybe the best dream we'd ever had. And even if it was just a dream, we were having it together and that made it worth it, didn't it?

Scene 27

Fool

Placard: '22nd of June, Waltham: King Richard Breaking his Promises to a Delegation of the Last Essex Rebels.'[64]

---

64   This scene is described in the chronicle by Froissart.

(**Katherine** *cowers as* **King, Walworth, Salisbury** *and an uncomfortable* **Fool** *enter*)

King

(*To audience, confident and assured*) 'Oh most vile and odious by land and sea, you who are not worthy to live when compared with the lords whom ye have attacked; you were and are serfs, and shall remain in bondage, not that of old, but in one infinitely worse, more vile without comparison. For as long as we live, and by God's help rule over this realm, we shall attempt by all our faculties, powers and means to make you such an example of offence to the heirs of your servitude as that they may have you before their eyes, as in a mirror, and you may supply them with a perpetual ground for cursing and fearing you, and fear to commit the like.'

Walworth

(*To* **Salisbury**, *impressed*) Contemptuous, vengeful, vicious.

Salisbury

(*Thoughtfully agreeing*) A king. (*Exchanges a knowing smile with* **Walworth** *then the audience. With heavy meaning*) For now.

King

(*As* **Salisbury** *exits, to* **Fool**) Eh? What's that?

Fool

(*Quickly dismissive*) Another story, your Majesty.

King

About me? (*A child again*) I hope it's a good one this time.

(**King** *waits expectantly for* **M3** *to become the throne. Confusion and debate between* **Fool** *and other* **Ms**. 'Are we doing that as well?' 'It won't take long.' 'Took Shakespeare two hours!' 'I said I'd be home in time to do the kid's dinner', etc.)

Walworth

(*Taking charge, seizes* **Katherine** *who maintains eye contact with him throughout*) Who is your rightful lord, peasant? (*Places his dagger* *at* **Katherine's** *throat*) Answer me!

King

(*Commandingly*) Walworth! Come.

(**Walworth** *releases* **Katherine.** *Nobles exit, then following,* **Elizabeth, Katherine**)

Scene 28

Fool

(*To audience*) Didn't think there'd be a happy one, did you?

> 'Man beware and be no Fool:
> Think upon the axe and of the tool!
> The block was hard, the axe was sharp,
> The fourth year of King Richard.'

Meet (**Fool** *summons* **Joan**, *handing her* **John Tyler's** *working tool. Giving* **Fool** *a strong look she stands as* **John Tyler** *at the beginning*) John Tyler's granddaughter, Elizabeth's child, Joan. Conceived in a silk sheeted, Savoy Palace, bunk up. Let's say her father, Edward, was one of the two or three thousand rounded up and butchered in the repression that followed the Revolt.[65] He could even have been one of the nineteen strung up from a single tree branch. (*Pretends to kick* **Sudbury's** *head*) Goal back for civilisation there. Vicious indeed, but there were *probably* sixty thousand that marched and more besides as resistance spluttered and sank across the country. Did Richard finally 'get' that he needed the peasants more than they needed him? Or was it nightmares tempered his lust for revenge? You can see this by the way, (*picks up* **Sudbury's** *head*) the real thing. At the church of St Gregory at Sudbury in Suffolk. Nice day out for the kids. (*Tosses the head to an* **M**) All of which leaves us with ... Good John Ball. (*Takes* **John Ball's** *signifier from their pocket*) A priest after all. They made him promise to keep his head down, gave him a cosy little parish in

---

[65] The Walsingham chronicle reports that around 7,000 were executed in the repression that followed the rising. Modern historical research has arrived at a lower figure. It is now thought that around 2,000 were killed.

Cornwall where he lived happily ever ...

King's official 1
There he is!

Fool
No? Oh well ...

King's official 2
Take him.

Scene 29

(**Fool** *struggles for Placard but* **M3** *has it already.* **Joan** *watches as* **John Ball/Fool** *is gently but firmly led into position by* **Ms 4** *and* **5**)

Mechanical 3

Placard: 'The Martyrdom of John Ball.'

(*Beatific expression on* **John Ball/Fool**'s *face, arms out as in crucifixion*)

Mechanical 5

(*Measured, detached, unemotional*) On the 15th of July 1381, in St Albans, John Ball, 'Hedgerow Priest', was hanged, drawn and quartered for High Treason.

Mechanical 4

John Ball *was* Highly Treasonous.

John Ball/Fool

I *did* lead an attack on the State's authority.

Mechanical 4

(*Glaring. 'Sorry, sorry!' from* **John Ball/Fool** *who resumes crucifixion pose*) He had been planning to do so for twenty years.

Mechanical 5

He was not sorry for it. (**Fool** *shakes head. Another glare and 'Sorry!'*)

Mechanical 4

He would encourage others in the future to do so too.

Mechanical 5

Should they get the chance.

(*Thumbs up from* **John Ball/Fool**. *Exasperation from* **Ms**. *'Last time, promise.' from* **John Ball/Fool**)

Mechanical 4

John Ball was hanged until nearly dead.

(*Challenging looks at* **John Ball/Fool** *from* **Ms**. *Nothing until they look away then a noose/tongue out, 'urgh!'*)

Mechanical 5

John Ball's balls and intestines were 'drawn' from his still living body and roasted in front of him. (**John Ball/Fool** *'helpfully' tugs out the first plastic sausage.* **M5** *tries to unemotionally 'draw' the rest but* **John Ball/Fool** *squirms 'That tickles!'*)

Mechanical 4

(*Emphatically*) John Ball's *head* was cut off, his body *hacked* into quarters. (**John Ball/Fool** *finally concedes they are 'dead'*)

Mechanical 5

King Richard had them sent to the four corners of his kingdom.

Mechanical 4

To impress upon the general population the importance of being non-treasonous.

Mechanical 5

King Richard had no more wars with France.

Mechanical 4

His downfall.

Mechanical 5

Serfdom in England ended fifty years after the Revolt. Centuries before the rest of Europe.[66]

Mechanical 4

There was no poll tax for another six hundred.

Mechanical 5

When we shout together.

Mechanical 4

They listen.

Scene 30

Mechanical 3

Placard: '1888: A Dream of John Ball and A King's Lesson, by William Morris.'[67]

(**Joan** *watches.* **John Ball**'s *arms are reverentially lowered, signifier in his hands*)

Mechanical 4

'John Ball, be of good cheer; for thou knowest, as I know, that the Fellowship of Man shall endure, however many tribulations it may have to wear through. It may well be that this bright day of summer, which is now dawning upon us, is no beginning of the day that shall be: but rather shall that day dawn be cold and grey and surly.'

Mechanical 5

'And yet by its light, shall we see things as they verily are, no longer enchanted by the gleam of the moon and the glamour of

---

66 The rising can be seen as the first of the great millenarian revolts that happened through Europe during the late Middle Ages, including the communist Hussite rebellions in Bohemia.

67 Taken from the final passage in William Morris's fictional drama based on the story of the Revolt.

the dream tide.'

Mechanical 3

'By such grey light shall valiant souls see remedy, and deal with it, a real thing that may be touched and handled.'

Mechanical 4

'And what shall it be, save that we shall be determined to be free; yea free as thou wouldst have them, when we shall have the fruits of the earth and the fruits of our toil thereon.'

Mechanical 3

'The time shall come, John Ball, when that dream of thine shall this one day be, shall be a thing that we shall talk of soberly, and as a thing soon to come about.'

Mechanicals 3, 4, 5

(**Mechanicals** *face* **John Ball**)

'Therefore, hast thou done well to hope it and thy name shall abide by thy hope in those days to come, and thou shall not be forgotten.'

(**Joan** *steps downstage, peasant tool swapped for a smartphone, becoming* **M2**, *scrolling and typing.* **M2** *stops, raises their eyes determinedly to the audience*)

Mechanical 2

(*To audience*) Matters cannot go well, nor ever shall until all things be held in common, when the lords shall be no more masters than ourselves. Therefore, I exalt you to consider that now the time is come, in which ye may, if ye will, cast off the yoke of bondage and recover liberty! When Adam delved and Eve span—who was then the gentleman?'

The End

Appendix I: Supporting organisations

The following trade union, cultural, and community organisations gave financial or promotional support for the *When Katherine Brewed* theatre project.

- Artists International Development Fund, British Council
- Liverpool Network Theatre
- International Herbert Marcuse Society
- Glastonwick Festival
- Northwest Region Trades Union Congress
- Southeast Region Trades Union Congress
- UNISON NW Region
- UCU NW Region
- UNISON Salford Care Organisation
- UNISON Sefton
- UNISON Environment Agency NW
- UNISON Manchester University Healthcare
- UNISON Burnley
- UNISON Southend
- UNISON Merseyside Police Staff Branch
- Liverpool Unite (construction)
- NEU Tower Hamlets
- Chelmsford Trades Union Council
- Coventry Trades Union Council
- Southend Trades Union Council
- East Ayrshire Trades Union Council
- Lancaster and Morecambe Trades Union Council
- Harlow Trades Union Council
- Norwich Trades Union Council
- Colchester Trades Union Council
- Leicester Trades Union Council
- Leeds Trades Union Council
- Camden Trades Union Council
- Inverness Trades Union Council
- Derby Trades Union Council
- Liverpool Trades Union Council

- Greenwich and Bexley Trades Union Council
- Lancashire Association of Trades Union Councils
- CWU, Greater Mersey and SW Lancashire
- Musicians' Union
- Equity NW Region

Appendix II: Permissions

When Katherine Brewed is a devised creation from a collaboration between John Cresswell and Mark O'Brien. It is based upon the book *When Adam Delved and Eve Span: A History of the Peasants' Revolt of 1381*, by Mark O'Brien.[1]

This play can only be staged and performed with written permission from Mark and John. Permission will be given generously with reference to the following considerations:

- Casting should prioritise diversity wherever possible, with any actor able to play any part, regardless of gender, ethnicity, sexuality, or ability/disability status.
- Performances should aim to reach all communities, but particularly those for whom opportunities to access theatre are restricted because of geographical, social, or economic limitations.
- Performances to be located in schools, trade union venues, or on estates will be considered particularly favourably.
- Ticket prices should be made affordable and intended to cover costs on a break-even-only basis.

Once permission is given, Mark and John will not seek to be involved in the preparations, rehearsals, or final staging.

Groups wishing to stage the play are encouraged to adapt it to suit their local circumstances, political context, and relevance to current events. This can be done with visual, audio, and staging techniques.

---

1 O'Brien, M. (2004), *When Adam Delved and Eve Span: A History of the Peasants' Revolt of 1381*, New Clarion Press.

Some elements of the script may be changed for this purpose. Changes can also be made for age-appropriateness and for school performances.

However, there can be no changes to the script that alter the substance of the play, its story, or its overall narrative and meaning.

Any script changes can only be made with written permission from Mark and John.

There is no permission fee.

Appendix III: Historical Characters

The purpose of the play is not to replicate the details of historical events. There are many things that happened that are not covered. There are also gaps in our modern knowledge of what exactly occurred and when, and much room for interpretation and dramatic license.

Rather, the aim is to capture the political intensity of the rising, the sense of historical possibility it opened up for the working people of England, and the lessons it contains for today.

Where chronicles are referred to, these are: *The Chronicles of England, France, Spain and the Adjoining Countries* (1405) by Jean Froissart;[2] the *Anonomalle Chronicle* (late 14th-century) by the monks of St Mary's Abbey at York;[3] the *Chronicles of England, Scotland and Ireland* (1577) by Raphael Holinshed;[4] and the *Chronicon Angliæ* (1388) by Thomas Walsingham of St Alban's Abbey.[5] Use is also made of The Oxford Dictionary of National Biography.

John Ball

John Ball was one of the many heretical itinerant clerics who were preaching the anti-Papal ideas of John Wycliffe, the Oxford theologian

---

2 Froissart, J. (*1901*), *The Chronicle of Froissart*, tr. by Bourchier, J., London, David Nutt, Volume II.
3 Anonymous (1870), *The Anonimalle Chronicle, 1333 to 1381: From a MS. Written at St Mary's Abbey, York*, ed. by Galbraith, V. H., Manchester University Press.
4 Holinshed, R. (2019), *Holinshed's Chronicles, England, Scotland and Ireland*, Volume III, Routledge.
5 Walsingham, T. (2012), *Chronicon Angliae, 1328–88*, ed. by Thompson, E. M., Cambridge University Press.

and philosopher. He had been active for 20 years before the Revolt, was known to the authorities, and had been imprisoned several times. He came into special prominence after his release from Maidstone gaol by Wat Tyler, and was involved in the final planning and communications for the rising.

Wat Tyler

Very little is known about Wat Tyler. We have no image of him. Despite speculation that he was from Essex or Kent, there is no biography or certain knowledge of his origins. It seems likely that he had some military experience and may have once been an officer in the English armies. His place in the historical record lasts for just ten days.

King Richard II (1367–1400)

Richard of Bordeaux was the French-speaking king of England from 1377 to 1399. He was the son of the Black Prince, Edward, Prince of Wales, who died before he could inherit the throne. The inheritance then passed to the ten-year-old Richard from his grandfather, so continuing the Plantagenet line. The break in direct inheritance and the presence of a boy-king caused John of Gaunt, brother to Edward III, to harbour his own ambitions to the throne. John of Gaunt's son, Henry Bolingbroke, would later invade England from France to depose Richard, and take the throne for himself in 1399.

Earl of Salisbury (1328–1397)

William Montagu, 2nd Earl of Salisbury, had been a commander in the armies of Edward III in France during the Hundred Years War. He had first come to prominence as a successful commander at the Battle of Poitiers in 1356. He had served his king well both as a soldier and a diplomat—negotiating the Treaty of Brétigny in 1360—and had been rewarded with his noble title and estates. He was an experienced military figure with a grasp of the strategy and tactics of major conflicts.

William Walworth (1322–1385)

Mayor of London 1380–81. Walworth had come to prominence as a figure in the Fishmongers' Guild under the reign of Edward III. Along with other merchants, he had made his fortune in corrupt business dealings and monopolies through ruthless guild rivalries, and by the manipulation of the King, who was by then in his late dotage, via the King's mistress, Alice Perrers. Walworth owned property on the south side of the Thames, renting much of it out to brothel-keepers.

Simon Sudbury (1316–1381)

Bishop of London 1361–1375 and Archbishop of Canterbury 1375–1381. Born in Suffolk, Sudbury studied at the University of Paris and became a chaplain of Pope Innocent VI, one of the Avignon rivals to Rome. He returned to England and became an ambassador for Edward III. He was responsible for the persecution of the popular Wycliffite preachers, and summoned Wycliffe himself to appear before him in 1378. As Archbishop of Canterbury, and with loyalty to John of Gaunt, he presided over an English church that was financially and morally corrupt. He was hated for this, as well as for his role in the creation and implementation of the third poll tax of Richard II.

John Tyler

Holinshed's Chronicle of England of 1577 tells us that the rising was started by John Tyler of Dartford. Whilst working on the roof of a nearby house, Tyler heard of the harassment of his family by poll tax collectors and the molestation of his daughter. We are told that he "caught his lathing staff[6] in his hand and ran reaking (riotously) home" and that in the altercation that followed, he "smote the collector with the lathing staff that the brains flew out of his head". And then, "great noise arose in the street, and the poor people, being glad, everyone prepared to support the said John Tyler."

Elizabeth Tyler

The daughter of John Tyler. 'Elizabeth' is an imagined name.

---

6   A lathing staff was a tiler's tool, with a metre-long handle with a sharp blade-like attachment.

Appendix IV: Fictitious Characters

The Fool

The figure of the Fool appears in royal courts across Europe. Their role varied from that of simple entertainment to that of significant influence with freedom to speak the truth in comic and satirical style. Their positions could be either perilous and short-lived or, sometimes, powerful and socially and politically successful; but far more often the former than the latter.

Katherine of Lakenheath

Katherine of Lakenheath is the central figure of the four rebel characters. She is an older woman and a brewer. Katherine is no fool and is looked to by the others for her shrewdness and wisdom. With dramatic license she is inspired by Katherine de Gamen of Lakenheath, one of only two named women to appear in the chronicles,[7] although she was not herself a brewer. Brewing was one of the very few trades by which a woman, such as our rebel Katherine, could achieve economic independence in this era.

Bartholomew Fletcher

An imagined ex-archer in the armies of Edward III. The bowmen of the English armies had achieved a fearsome reputation at the Battle of Crécy (1346) and the Battle of Poitiers (1356), both being famous victories for the English armies.

Godwin Rolfe

Rolfe is an imagined character who has served time with John Ball in the Maidstone gaol, one of the prisons of Simon Sudbury, Archbishop of Canterbury.

Joan

Adult daughter of Elizabeth Tyler, grand-daughter of John Tyler.

---

7   Johanna Ferrour of Rochester also played a key role in leading the rebels to the Tower of London.

Poll tax collectors

These were the hated figures who represented all that was wrong with English society. It was the poll tax collectors who arrived at the villages to demand the tax, carry out the puberty test, and report evasion and other forms of resistance back to the local magistrates.

They Stayed at Home

Every village would have had such characters, without whom village subsistence might have collapsed.

About the Team

Alessandra Tosi was the managing editor for this book.

Proofreading by Lila Fierek and Lucy Barnes.

Jeevanjot Kaur Nagpal designed the cover. The cover was produced in InDesign using the Fontin font.

Jeremy Bowman typeset the book in InDesign and produced the paperback and hardback editions. The main text font is Tex Gyre Pagella and the heading font is Californian FB. Jeremy also produced and created the PDF and EPUB editions.

The conversion to the HTML edition was performed with epublius, an open-source software which is freely available on our GitHub page at https://github.com/OpenBookPublishers.

This book was peer-reviewed by Prof Lynn Arner, Brock University, Rebecca Hillman, University of Exeter, and an anonymous referee. Experts in their field, these readers give their time freely to help ensure the academic rigour of our books. We are grateful for their generous and invaluable contributions.

This book need not end here...

Share

All our books — including the one you have just read — are free to access online so that students, researchers and members of the public who can't afford a printed edition will have access to the same ideas. This title will be accessed online by hundreds of readers each month across the globe: why not share the link so that someone you know is one of them?

This book and additional content is available at
https://doi.org/10.11647/OBP.0456

Donate

Open Book Publishers is an award-winning, scholar-led, not-for-profit press making knowledge freely available one book at a time. We don't charge authors to publish with us: instead, our work is supported by our library members and by donations from people who believe that research shouldn't be locked behind paywalls.

Join the effort to free knowledge by supporting us at
https://www.openbookpublishers.com/support-us

We invite you to connect with us on our socials!

BLUESKY
@openbookpublish.
bsky.social

MASTODON
@OpenBookPublish@
hcommons.social

LINKEDIN
open-book-publishers

Read more at the Open Book Publishers Blog
https://blogs.openbookpublishers.com

You may also be interested in:

After the Miners' Strike
A39 and Cornish Political Theatre versus Thatcher's Britain: Volume 1
Paul Farmer and Mark Kilburn, with a Preface by Rebecca Hillman

https://doi.org/10.11647/OBP.0329

Theatre and War
Notes from the Field
Nandita Dinesh

https://doi.org/10.11647/OBP.0099

Chronicles from Kashmir
An Annotated, Multimedia Script
Nandita Dinesh

https://doi.org/10.11647/OBP.0223

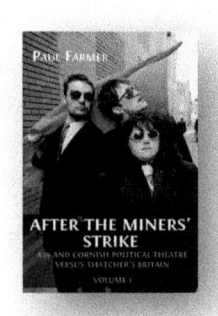